faith
intersections

faith. intersections

Christians Listen to...

a Muslim

a Scientologist

a Buddhist

a Mormon

and Others

Compiled by
Matt
Zimmer

BEACON HILL PRESS
OF KANSAS CITY

Copyright 2010 by Beacon Hill Press of Kansas City

ISBN 978-0-8341-2467-7

Printed in the
United States of America

Cover Design: Doug Bennett
Interior Design: Sharon Page

Library of Congress Cataloging-in-Publication Data

    Faith intersections : Christians listen to— a Muslim, a Scientologist, a Buddhist, a
Mormon, and others / compiled by Matt Zimmer.
         p. cm.
    Includes bibliographical references (p.   ).
    ISBN 978-0-8341-2467-7 (pbk.)
    1. Christianity and other religions. 2. Religious adherents—United States—
Interviews. I. Zimmer, Matt, 1970-
    BR127.F344 2010
    261.2—dc22

                                 2010023169

10 9 8 7 6 5 4 3 2 1

Contents

Introduction and Acknowledgments

Listening to one another and speaking only when necessary is a discipline few practice well. If not closely guarded, it can too easily become merely a social inconvenience that a person must endure before interjecting his or her own opinion. Listening in this way is not really listening, since no thought is given to what the other person says. I've been guilty of this on numerous occasions. I will "listen" to someone but not really try to understand or discover that person's heart.

This book is about really listening, about trying to hear the hearts of people who have different beliefs from our own and from each other. It is a book designed to help us listen closer to people in order to gain a better understanding of who they are and why they believe as they do. This book is not about converting people to Christianity or coercing those who believe differently into the Christian faith. It is rather a book that seeks to give us a peek into real conversations so that we can look within ourselves and try to discover how we can have similar conversations with someone who might be Buddhist, Jewish, or without any belief in God or a higher power at all.

As these conversations unfold, they will provide some historical background for each belief system, and that in turn will improve the quality and depth of our conversations with people holding similar beliefs. Because there are so many religious battlefronts in our world, we need to just consider what it means to truly listen to our fellow human beings and to really care about them. As we do, I think we will find that God's gracious presence will shine through our conversations and relationships and maybe even eventually lead a friend to see God in a new light.

My many thanks go out to all our chapter writers and to those with whom they visited to obtain these conversations. These writers are teaching us how to listen to the stories and hearts of others as real people and not as trophies to be won.

Finally, I would like to thank Bonnie Perry and the Beacon Hill Press team for their willingness to explore the idea of using shared stories as a medium for learning from different faith systems. The stories we hear from each other can teach us so much about faith, family, and friends. Our own stories mold us into who we are, but when shared they can help us become something better if we just take the time to really listen.

—*Matt Zimmer*

one Listening to a Former Christian

Darrel Harvey

In the last year I have navigated some interesting waters. I sailed out of the sea of paid professional ministry and into the stream of missional living in the marketplace. After twenty-four years of church work, I bought a small coffee shop and I am learning to live among people as a friend and peer. Speaking and listening to others, not from the bridge as a captain, but on the deck as a fellow traveler has been good for me.

In this new venture, I have found people who are quite free about sharing their beliefs and questions, telling their stories and secrets, and baring their hopes and wounds. Each day I have conversations with people from all sorts of faith backgrounds. Some are casual; others are passionate. But I haven't found anyone yet who doesn't have an opinion on religion in general and Christianity in particular. To put it simply, most of the people I am getting to know have a tenderness toward God but reservations about the church. I remember thinking, *I am surrounded by potential candidates for this chapter. How will I choose the right person?* It was a bit overwhelming. I knew my contribution to the book would require more than a chat with a new acquaintance.

I shared my dilemma with a longtime friend. He was excited for me. This did not surprise me, because he has always encouraged me in my writing. But what came next from him caught me off guard. "I'll do it," he said. "What?" I replied with a nervous chuckle. "I'll be your person who has walked away from Christianity."

Throughout our friendship Scott has expressed his frustration with the widening gap between what Jesus taught and modeled and the way Western Christians live and behave. We have spent hours venting our disappointment with corporate religion and wondering what Christ thinks about the things done in his name. But now Scott was identifying himself as a former Christian, and this was a new step for him.

Our Friendship

Let me back up. I met Scott as an eighteen-year-old college freshman, but we didn't really get acquainted until ten years later. My wife and I were considering moving to a new city, church, and assignment. Scott was a part of the group I was having lunch with during the process. I remembered him right away from college, but this time as we talked and joked, I immediately sensed the spark of prospective friendship. I am always amazed that God has given human beings the ability to sense the potential for connection and relationship. We meet (or remeet) someone and instantly things start firing in our heart and brain that say, *I like this person. We connect. What might God be up to here?*

My wife and I decided to accept the assignment and make the move. Not long after our arrival I realized Scott and I had similar interests, senses of humor, upbringing, and frustrations. Over the years Scott has become a great friend, never avoiding an opportunity to uplift, challenge, confront, or affirm. To this day he continues to live out what Ralph Waldo Emerson meant when he said, "I do not wish to treat friendships daintily, but with roughest courage. When they are real, they are not glass threads or frost-work, but the solidest thing we know."[1] I cannot think of anything we have not talked about. He has permission to ask me any question he wants, and he has given me the same privilege. When we talk, everything is on the table—God, marriage, parenting, sports, and the condition of our hearts.

Scott and I are true friends, and the conversation that follows comes from a friendship that was birthed in ordinary circumstances, grown in the soil of our shared interests, and refined in the furnace of pain. It is a friendship that continues to grow through the foggy landscape of questioning and doubt.

Unchristian

Before we go too far, we need to understand what the words "Christian" and "Christianity" mean to Scott: "Currently, when I hear or use the term 'Christianity,' I think of the [different] institutions that bear the name church. In other words, I think of Christianity in very broad and sweeping ways. Yes, I know there [are many variations] within the tradition of Christianity between the many doctrinal camps; yet with very few exceptions most churches are in the business of selling some sort of salvific product."

That word "product" struck me. Scott is not the only non-Christian to imply that the church looks more like a distributor of religious goods and services than the dynamic movement we see depicted in scripture. It caused me to think back to some of the conversations I had with Christians who visited my church as they searched for a new one. At some point the discussion would get around to them saying, "What do you have for us and our children?" Many were not looking for a mission to give themselves to but a new religious sweater to try on. We on the inside need to acknowledge that more often than not, our unbelieving neighbors are right. We have overpromised and underdelivered. We have lowered the bar. We have tamed a dangerous movement. Scott said, "Let me put it another way: Christianity is much more concerned about increasing market share by getting people saved than in wrestling with statements attributed to Jesus [that] have deeply political, economic, and [worldwide] implications. Let me say it even another way: I think Christianity would [prefer to save] people who love/care poorly than to acknowledge people who love well but don't embrace Jesus as the only way."

Scott did not grow up on the fringes of Christianity. He is a third-generation member of an evangelical denomination, a graduate of a Christian college, and a former ordained minister. His experiences with us go back as far as his memory, so his opinions of Christians are vivid, colorful, and moving:

I love some Christians deeply, and I have no appreciation for the beliefs or [lifestyles] of others. The same could be said of any people group. [Some] have not thought very deeply about what they say they believe and therefore are very inconsistent in orthodoxy and orthopraxis. As a whole I believe Christians practice a religion of convenience and comfort. I agree with Gandhi's assessment that Christians are more invested in practicing a religious experience than in living out the radical and demanding teachings of their Man-God. The face of Christianity, the image most people [think of], is not one of wondrous graciousness, economic criticism, nonjudgmentalism, rationality, [and so on]. There is a reason for this, and it isn't simply due to [the media's] portrayal. Hypocrisy and dishonesty is rampant.

While Scott's comments about some of the Christians he knows stings, I can't help but notice the respect, even reverence, he has for Jesus. I have suggested that his frustration with the church is directly linked to his admiration for Jesus. I think he appreciates my optimism concerning his spiritual condition, but he does not act as if he buys it. However, this does lead us back to what Scott says about the simplicity of Jesus' teaching: "From my perspective, most of what Christianity is so heavily invested in theologically is rooted primarily in Pauline influence and second- to fourth-century politics. Jesus and his teachings are viewed [backward] through this grid, thereby distorting and minimizing his core message." I reflected on my own upbringing and training. Setting aside Christ's birth, death, and resurrection, I was much more familiar with the writings of Paul and the teachings of the church than the life of Jesus.

Scott concedes, "I'm not sure how to completely determine what that core message is; however, I am certain it is much less bulky and much more radical than the current, overall message [of Christianity]." In his opinion Christianity has repeatedly focused on the wrong things for the past two thousand years:

> After two thousand years claiming to speak for God and claiming to be empowered by God through the Holy Spirit and claiming to have the keys to a fulfilling life, Christianity has yet to bring about anything that appears to be close to the kingdom Jesus described. Christians are just as likely to hate, to cheat, and to judge as those who are not Christians. If Christianity were true, then I would [expect] that

the present economic and political powers would be challenged [because Christians would] no longer [be] playing by their rules. If Christianity were true, then I would expect that there would be graciousness, forgiveness, compassion, justice, and mercy left in its wake. If Christianity were true, then resources and time would be spent addressing what [seem] to be bigger problems than programs, buildings, and alternative recreational choices. It seems to me that addressing poverty, injustice, [and] inequality would not be [a] side [program] of Jesus' followers or [an] exception to the usual [program] of telling people they are lost.

In the spring of 2008 I had the opportunity to speak at a pastors' gathering. It was an opportunity to join the conversation on where the church should head and what should shape our ministry in the twenty-first century. I knew Scott would be helpful, and I could not wait to get his input. I also knew it would be an opportunity for him to unpack his thoughts further on the core message of Christ and the ministry of the church. After all, it is easy to pick apart any religion, but to make suggestions on how to fulfill "our" mission is quite another matter.

We e-mailed back and forth and talked on the phone several times about the topic and the event. While he has always had great credibility with me, and his voice consistently rings loudly in my heart, his first paragraph in one e-mail got my attention:

To be honest, I nearly talked myself out of giving any feedback because I don't really believe your audience wants to do anything differently beyond [making] programming changes. Maybe that should be Part 1—I've got something to say, but you don't really want to deal with it. That's harsh, I'm sure. So let me say it differently. Since I am most likely apostate at best and a pagan at worst, I don't think I have any credibility to say, "Your theology, worldview, and praxis [are inadequate], and you'll never reach the growing numbers of nonreligious until you seriously reconsider what you are about."

I started to think seriously about who I am and what the church I led was about. I wondered how much the birth and growth of the institutional church and the rise of the church growth movement had affected me. How far have I drifted from the picture Jesus painted in his words and life? How often are my choices as a leader driven by a desire for more "market share" instead of life transformation? My conversation with Scott would not only be helpful in addressing a group of pastors but also be critical in shaping my ministry in the twenty-first century. As we talked, a metaphor surfaced. Scott said, "Set a larger table."

He continued,

I believe this idea returns us to the early church's seeming preoccupation with hospitality . . . , the image of Jesus offending the religious by who he ate with, and Paul's encouragement to the "strong" to accommodate the sensibilities of the weak. From my past experience as an "insider" and now as an "outsider" with increasingly secular tastes, I would never describe [those in my former denomination] as people who are comfortable eating, let alone opening their homes, with just anybody figuratively or literally. I know how you all, clergy and laity alike, talk; after all, I talked right along with you about sinners, and I know that an invitation to your home is more like being invited to learn about a tremendous business opportunity, like Amway, than to a party. I'm sure everyone is not like this, but it is the exceptional and not the normal [church member] who doesn't see the "lost" as projects or opportunities or offensive.

Christians have small tables where only close family [are] invited to come and sit without fear of embarrassment or correction or judgment. You all may think you set a big table, but your actions and attitudes convey a different message. We know that our preferences, political positions, and social choices offend you and in turn encourage you to tell us how we need to change or risk going to hell. So, why would we want to sit at a table with you? In other words, we know you don't like us for ourselves, just as we are, so we'll take the lead and prevent making you any more uncomfortable than you already are.

As I recall (and cling to) your master's level of grace, . . . his demand of those calling themselves disciples to express a similar level of grace was huge! His grace was big enough, his table large enough, to be offensive to even the minimally proper. In short, he lacked good taste and didn't seem to give a rip about what others thought [about him] . . . sitting with those of disreputable character. I don't know if he enjoyed it, but I sure want to believe he did. So as leaders in his movement, why not set about extending grace to his level by inviting us all to sit at a very big table where the notions of who can eat freely or not [are] very, very blurry? Why not examine in [yourselves] why you find us so hard to truly embrace and ask your God to create in you a genuine affection for something more than our souls?

Yes, I am asking you to keep your nose out of my personal business—you haven't earned the right. Yes, I am telling you that I am not likely to change my behaviors simply because you tell me they are offensive to your God. Yes, I will continue to misbehave long after we have coffee together. So, I know what I am suggesting to you is very difficult to stomach and highly unlikely.

However, I will be happy to raise my beer to your coke and to share a good meal and to laugh at our foible-filled stories and to debate social policy and to go on long walks through narrow canyons, if I know you completely accept me—period—no strings attached. Are you willing to make your table that big—really? Are you willing to call your own out when their tables are small? Are you willing to put on hold your need to convert me so we can simply enjoy a good burger and basketball game? Are you willing to make your table that big for the likes of me to sit at?

If the purpose of this book is to help us listen to our unbelieving neighbors, friends, coworkers, and relatives, then these questions have to be considered on an individual and corporate level. But I also hear Scott asking us larger questions: Are we truly Trinitarian? Do we believe in the Holy Spirit? Do we trust him to do his work? Do I see my role of being a friend, walking alongside people who might make me uncomfortable, as sacred and enough, while allowing him to do the rest?

Scott and I have had many conversations about personal evangelism. Since he grew up in the church, he has seen and heard it all. As a teenager he served as a leader in the local youth ministry. He has been trained in personal evangelism. He has given altar calls. He has seen all sorts of tactics used on individuals and crowds to solicit a particular response. Now he is on the other side of the issue and quite vocal about our attempts at soul winning.

I asked him what we could do: "You know the tension that we (those of us from an evangelistic tradition) live in. How do we address this challenge? How can we be faithful to our understanding of the Great Commission in a post-Christian and postmodern culture?"

Scott responded,

One thing you could do: Value and focus on [my] present life more than my future eternity. I'm sorry, but we skeptics don't care as much about heaven or hell as you do. It's not that we want to change your mind about how great [life] is going to be after you're dead, but eternal life is not something we think about in general and don't trust specifically. Please forgive us, but we are really tangible people with a "seeing is believing" mind-set and [we were] raised in an ever-increasing technological world that has its roots in empiricism. I mean, you wouldn't ask us to believe again . . . that the world was created literally in [seven] days or that the sun rotated around the earth or that schizophrenics were possessed by evil entities, [would you?].

To be honest, you'd be better off not bringing up the subject to us for more compelling reasons—[because] it causes us to feel superior and [because] we don't have anything to learn from you. Why? First, we can't buy into the logic that a divine being who loves us more than the universe itself (so you all say) could ever bring himself/herself/itself to [hand] us over to demonic waterboarding. Yeah, yeah, I can recall the way you get around this by making it our failure to decide—fair enough; but that begs the question. Forget about the obviously logical problems with people who deal with mental illness [and] personality disorders, [who] live in third-world countries, or who are immersed in non-Christian cultures, [and so on]. Instead, all you really have to do is ask any parent off the street if [he or she] would stand by idly and allow [his or her] child to be tortured because of [the child's] own stupidity.

Do you see my point? If your peers still aren't convinced, tell them to ask that same parent a second time, but this time have them really ramp it up by telling the parent that [the] child's stupidity was rampant, that she broke [her parent's] heart multiple times in the face of [her parent's] pleas to do differently with her life, and [that] she repeatedly went against [her parent's] good advice, then ask the parent if then [he or she would] be [OK] with an eternity of woe for that kid. Yeah, yeah, I know, if I were holy and pure and transcendent, the decision would be easier—but if that's holiness, then the CIA must be dishing it out in the truckloads and I want to be as far away from it as possible. Honestly, we feel pretty arrogant about this point and truly believe our position holds the high moral ground—sorry; let's just agree to disagree.

Second, I'm sure your compatriots don't mean it, but we have come to see your use of heaven and hell as a type of religious boogeyman. It comes off as a sales pitch used to scare us into buying a universal life insurance policy immediately or, worse, as a way of wearing us down [as] a Kirby vacuum salesman [would do]. "Yes, yes, I'll take Jesus and heaven, now will you please get out of my living room!" Darrel, we don't care, we aren't convinced, we don't want to go someplace that excludes the likes of us, and we definitely think if that is the best you have to offer, it's a weak reason to become religious.

Perhaps most importantly, telling me about hell in our future does nothing about the hell [in] our present. As a group, we tend to be most concerned about the here and now. We agree with you—there is a lot of suffering in this world. Where we differ is that we think it will take a whole lot more than going to church to bring comfort to the hurting. I know this probably isn't fair, but doesn't Jesus' teachings talk more about abundant living and God's kingdom now than about eternal retirement locations after death? There is enough hell on earth to keep your Jesus-machine working overtime on things like hunger, poor education, racism, militarism, planet extinction, and overall human rights. These are issues that many of us feel deeply about, and we have [gotten] to the point where we don't think the government or big business is going to address them in creative, honest, or earnest ways. Yes, I'll be honest with you, we are as guilty as the next American in helping to create and perpetuate these global (and neighborhood) problems—we are selfish, consumeristic, hateful, wasteful, and as likely as the next guy to drop a bomb on our enemies if threatened.

Listen, many of us are clutching [on] to hope "out here," and we are wanting and waiting to be inspired, to be challenged, and to see and believe that as a people "we can do better than we have." Does Jesus have anything to say about this? Would he go about addressing these problems any differently than we are? Could your congregations model for us [what] an alternative approach to living looks [like] in the here and now? Please quit trying to save me from hell, and show me the power of the gospel to address poverty, hatred, divisiveness, suffering, [and so on]. Seeing something like that occurring before our very eyes would be more compelling than streets of gold, and [it would be] something we would get behind and give our energies to whether we ever bought into that insurance plan of yours.

I wonder what you, the readers, are thinking right now. Have you written my friend off as a malcontent or someone who is misguided or disgruntled or bitter? Or are you listening? I am thinking of what a gift I have in a friend like Scott. He reminds me that many seekers, skeptics, and cynics are looking for evidence and encouragement that there is a better way to live. He is looking for good news. Good news for today. Good news that life is worth living. Scott's presence in my life also causes me to evaluate whether I am clinging to the Christian faith or only a cultural expression of the faith.

Most of our conversation thus far has been about Scott's impressions of us—Christians and Christianity. It would be unfair for me to leave you thinking that all he was willing to do was unload on our beliefs and behaviors. He was just as open about sharing his views on spirituality. Here is what our conversation was like:

DARREL: So what is it all about? What is the purpose of life? Why are we here?

SCOTT: To live and love fully.

DARREL: What do you mean by that?

SCOTT: By "love" I mean to care well for our neighbors . . . local, national, and international. The term is more akin to the word "agape" and carries with it the idea that I am to be invested in compassion, justice, mercy, and equality.

DARREL: How is that going?

SCOTT: I hope I am gracious, forgiving, wise. I hope I listen well. I hope I am loyal.

DARREL: How do your beliefs influence your daily life?

SCOTT: I hope I am learning to love better. I hope I am living more consistently with my beliefs about caring well for others.

DARREL: How do your beliefs affect your relationships with others?

SCOTT: My lack of believing about Christianity affects my wife to some degree, and maybe even my friends. For her, I believe there is some level of anxiety created by my disbelief and agnosticism. However, I also think my humanistic leanings are appreciated by her. I believe she would say I am maturing and becoming a better person. Of course, she doesn't understand why I can't do both! Truly, if I could make myself believe, I would. I keep looking at the emperor, telling myself he has clothes on, but each time I open my eyes I see a naked man. Oddly, several of my friends who are Christians have suggested I am living more closely aligned to the teachings of Jesus than ever. I don't know. I hope so, but I don't think they have an absolutely clear picture.

Having a friend like Scott has taken away the oversimplified notion that Christians are the good people, as if we are the only ones who are upright, honest, and honorable. I have had the benefit of watching him in different situations. I have seen him deal with challenging people. We have been in situations where integrity could have been put on the shelf. I have witnessed him consistently choose the difficult path of goodness. So to put it bluntly, I asked him, "What ethical principles do you live by?" Here is his response:

On this point, I would agree with the Humanist Manifesto:

Ethical values are derived from human need and interest as tested by experience. Humanists ground values in human welfare shaped by human circumstances, interests, and concerns and extended to the global ecosystem and beyond. We are committed to treating each person as having inherent worth and dignity, and to making informed choices in a context of freedom consonant with responsibility.[2]

As we have talked over the years of our friendship and more specifically during the last few months, I can see how this philosophy guides Scott's ideas and life. He takes seriously the impact of his choices and their effects. Not for some eternal reward but because of the immediate consequences and benefits. I made sure to ask him specifically about eternity and destiny:

DARREL: What effect do your choices have on your destiny?

SCOTT: If by destiny, you mean "tomorrow," then my choices have real and ongoing effects that I must deal with on a daily basis. If by "destiny" you mean "afterlife," then my choices will be something those who knew me must deal with at some level.

DARREL: What about heaven, hell, karma, some sort of check and balance in the universe? Do you believe in any of that?

SCOTT: Nope.

I then asked him, "What do you believe about God, human freedom, the natural world, human relationships?" and he gave this reply:

"Believe" is the right word, because I have no actual knowledge of a divine being outside of time, space, and natural law. At this point, I am probably located somewhere between agnosticism and atheism. The idea of God as typically defined by most if not all religions is untenable to me. Currently the

most accurate description of where I am is that provided by
Dawkins: "I cannot know for certain but I think God is very
improbable. . . ."[3] Christians would probably suggest that my
failure to believe is a lack of faith or simply hostility. Perhaps.
However, I have tried to [believe], to embrace, to convince
myself that there is something divine and spiritual. The best
way to describe it is that I don't seem to have the mechanism
to allow me to truly believe. I could say "I believe" or "I have
faith," but I would know, deep down, that at heart I am very
doubtful. This is not to say I am closed to having my mind
changed or having the mechanism to believe added; but it
will require something I have not been able to muster up for
the past [forty-plus] years.

Human freedom—yes and no. This is a very philosophical
question. We are not completely free to do whatever we want;
we are not free from the "influence" of culture, economic systems, dominant worldviews, or our genetics. However, I think
I have the ability to make choices on a daily basis, to say yes
or no, to invest my energies in one direction or another. The
ability to think seems to imply a level of human freedom.

The natural world exists and can be encountered. It
should be protected and partnered with versus taken advan-
tage of and used up. The natural world is all that exists. If
something exists that cannot be seen or discerned, it is because we have not discovered or developed far enough to see
or discern it. For instance, the idea of existence at the atomic
level was posited long before it was actually proven to exist. I
believe, along with most physicists, that there are many more
dimensions than the handful we currently experience (e.g.,
worm holes). These dimensions are still part of the natural

world. Knowledge of the world is derived by observation, experimentation, and rational analysis.

Humans are social by nature and find meaning in relationships. Relationships are central to our becoming and living. We are relational beings that desire for and benefit from intimacy, friendship, brotherhood, and community. The evil done through systems (e.g., economic, political, social) and individuals is the result, in part, of ignoring our "relatedness" and our "commonality."

I then asked Scott, "How does your position help you to understand suffering, crises, and why bad things happen to good people?" He responded by saying, "Why do good things happen to bad people? . . . 'Bad things' do not have a will or intent; the bad in life is not discriminate but dependent on genetics, context, chance, [and so on]. 'Bad' is not an entity. 'Bad' is a word used to describe a subjective sense of what is not desirable by an individual or a group. Sometimes things defined as 'bad' are later embraced as the 'best thing to ever happen to me' and vice versa."

I hope you resist the temptation to assume my friend Scott is arrogant. I know that he wrestles with these issues daily. He weighs his decisions of right and wrong, how he spends his money, and what he gives his time to more conscientiously than many Christians I know. He openly admits, "Too many of my decisions are based in self-interest, self-protection, and selfishness. Hopefully I utilize wisdom, consider how my choices might affect those I love, and examine whether my decision is aligned with what I say I believe."

This project has taken our friendship to new places. We have talked about familiar topics from totally different vantage points. In one such conversation I said, "We Christians talk a lot about worship. For several years you and I talked about it programmatically and even worked on planning worship. I wonder now, how do you worship? What does worship mean to you?" Scott replied,

Worship for me is those moments when I am absolutely present; when I am awake to the moment I am in—listening, breathing, absorbing, living. I am not present very often and believe this should be remedied! [I think.] The solution to becoming more mindful is likely to come through contemplation and practicing mindfulness. I suppose worship is also about those moments of joy, discovery, and speechlessness that sometimes meet you through the course of a day/lifetime. Examples include a hug from your child, forgiveness from a spouse, falling to the ground next to a brother [and] gasping for air after pushing [yourself] to the limit, and seeing graciousness.

I recently sat with Scott in a worship service. We went to hear a mutual friend preach. The music was good. The message was inspired and powerful. Communion was served. I remember being particularly moved at one point. Scott noticed, leaned over, and said, "You know you are loved, right?" "Yes," I whispered. Volumes were communicated in those six words, but I think even more was communicated in what went unsaid. That is a snapshot of my friendship with Scott. I have been surprised by grace, kingdom living, and acceptance more often in my relationship with him than in my relationship with those who are certain of their faith. I am truly blessed to have a friend like him. I am glad I am not God (and you are too). I am glad I do not have the responsibility of rendering some sort of final judgment, for it is hard to imagine a heaven without Scott.

two Listening to a Rabbi

Matt Zimmer

On a cold and rainy day I was so glad that my meeting with Rabbi Alan was inside a warm Starbucks coffee shop. I was also glad to be at Starbucks because I knew it would be one place where a Christian pastor with Wesleyan roots and a Jewish rabbi could find something in common to begin an in-depth conversation. We both liked drinking hot beverages on wet and chilly days, and that shared enjoyment was enough to open the way to a most unforgettable discussion about our different worldviews.

Meeting Rabbi Alan Cohen was like meeting a rich uncle for the first time. He was rich in knowledge, rich in orderly living, and richly devoted to his Jewish faith. I was entranced by his presence throughout our talk. As we conversed, he had many profound things to say about life, Judaism, and Jesus.

Rabbi Alan's background is exceptional. Originally from Cleveland, Rabbi Alan spent thirty-six years as a congregational rabbi in what he considered to be the conservative denomination of the Jewish tradition. For the past nineteen years he was congregational rabbi at Beth-Shalom in Kansas City until he retired in June 2008. He currently serves as director of Interreligious Affairs for the Jewish Community Relations Bureau/American Jewish Committee. His main role these days is creating religious harmony in the community along with combating anti-Semitism in the urban setting. He's initiated a three-year plan for these objectives and is in the middle of year two as of this writing.

Our conversation got under way as I asked my first question:

MATT: So, rabbi, what is the driving idea or philosophy that shapes your worldview and how you live your life every day?

ALAN: Two [scripture passages] really shape how I live each and every day. The first is Genesis 1, the second Leviticus 19. The first passage reminds me that God creates and every human being is made in the image of God. My attitude isn't like, "There's a Gentile or there's a Jew; there's a suburban white man or a black woman." No, I try to see God's created without all the labels humankind uses. The second passage from Leviticus reminds me that I need to love others as I love myself. The "if/then" role of Genesis and Leviticus means that if people are made in the image of God, and love and respect for others is the highest of my values, then my purpose is to work for a world where people respect each other, [to] work to eliminate injustice, discrimination, and so on. This is why we are here, to make the world a better place to live, to repair the world where it is broken.

MATT: Rabbi, what does worship mean to you?

ALAN: Worship to me means prayer that communicates with God. Prayer is a verb that calls for introspection. Prayer is as much about communicating with oneself as it is talking and communicating with God. I would say, too, that the Jewish ritual, to me, is not restrictive but in fact liberating because as I move with the rhythms of the Jewish calendar, the days I celebrate, the foods I eat or do not eat, the prayers I pray—all tie me closer and closer to God.

MATT: What do you believe about God and the human condition of sin and human freedom?

ALAN: We are created with free will. Genesis 2 is not about punishment but about consequences.

MATT: So, in this way perhaps Jews are very much in harmony with Christians who, like me, are of the Wesleyan heritage? We believe humankind does have free will and that we can come to God or turn from God by our own choosing.

ALAN: Yes, this is very much what I believe.

MATT: Why do you believe the way you do, Alan?

ALAN: I'm a product of my parents, education, and social mind-set [all of which believe that] the human being is not the center of the universe. This makes more sense to me than believing that I am the center of the universe. I mean, look at us humans. We walk into a room [and] flip a switch, and light illuminates the room. Something like that, as simple as it is, gives us as humans a high sense of accomplishment. So from there to the great technologies we've developed we can easily see ourselves as central players in this universe. *Shabbat,** though, means that I say I'm not the center of the universe. There is a Creator; he is in

---

**Shabbat,* meaning "rest," is the Jewish Sabbath, or rest from work, observed on the seventh day of the week (from Friday evening to Saturday evening).

charge and I'm not. This is what I was taught from a young age and why I believe what I do.

MATT: Switching gears a bit, Alan, can you tell me what happens to your soul when you die?

ALAN: Physically I go back to the earth. Jews bury each other in wooden boxes because we are made from the dust and return to the dust, and the wooden box enables this returning process. As far as our soul, we have a soul. This is [reflected] in Genesis. We are the only created beings with God's breath in us. The soul is immortal. [Where will my soul] be? I can't tell you that. I know that souls will be reunited in the afterlife with friends and family and that the soul is always there, but where, I'm not sure.

MATT: Back to a not so heavy topic. How do your beliefs influence your daily life?

ALAN: Beginning when I rise and thank God for restoring my soul (this is the *Modeh Ani**), I am in prayer with God. Then I follow the rhythms of three prayer services daily. The calendar rhythms are vital to me as well. Daily and annual ritual motivates me in my behavior so that I function with a set purpose—not helter-skelter—it keeps me on course.

I would also say that *Shabbat* helps me think again that what I did in the previous week starts with Genesis. *Shabbat* is a fresh Genesis for me.

MATT: So ritual is not a restrictive thing for you but a life-giving element to your faith.

ALAN: Yes, exactly.

MATT: In regard to ethics, what do you believe about a final judgment of the human race?

Modeh Ani, meaning "I give thanks," is the first prayer Jews recite for the day.

ALAN: Jews focus less on the final judgment of the human race and more on the judgment of individuals. "How did I behave toward other human beings?" This is what I will be judged on in large part. "Was I the best Alan Cohen I could have been?" This is the final-judgment question. We Jews have no sense of Christian "left behind" imagery. We will simply be judged by our actions on this planet by how we lived our lives with God and with other human beings.

MATT: What are Jews you know saying about the Christian church? Is there any feeling among the Jews that the Christian church has lost its way, or is there a sense of renewed spirit and purpose concerning the Christian church?

ALAN: Let me say first that I feel the turning point for the Christian church concerning Jewish-Christian relations came at Vatican II in 1965. This was a monumental event [because] I now feel [that for] the past 45 years . . . Jews generally feel [from Christians] an openness that Judaism is a valid way to behave. That being said, both Jews and Christians are dealing with fundamental issues in society today. Therefore, most Jews feel that religion in general is a positive force that can make life meaningful. There's a valuable lesson for Jews and Christians from the weeping of Ishmael in Genesis 21. This boy and his mother were cast out, and we read that God heard his cries where he was at. We as Jews and Christians should strive to go where people are at, because they are crying. To be even more specific to your question, I look at [a Christian] like I would look at any other human. I see certain differences in belief, but I see a person trying to make the world a better place.

MATT: Here's my final question, Alan. It's the "elephant in the room" question. How do you view Jesus, and how would Jews in general view him?

ALAN: First, let's be clear. Jesus was born, lived, and died a Jew. Jesus and his followers were one of many Jewish paths that people could walk at the time of his life on earth. He was a rabbi who had his followers and was very much a part of the Jewish world. Christianity [emerged] as a separate path from Judaism in large part because of Paul. Jesus was a teacher, [a] rabbi, a part of the Jewish world, but not the Messiah as Christians believe he was. That being said, what Jesus preached and taught while on earth has nothing to do with some of the anti-Semitism that has been felt on many Good Fridays of the past.

MATT: Alan, I couldn't agree more with that last statement.

What We Hear

Alan and I could have talked on forever. After our conversation, I had a yearning to adopt some of the features of Alan's lifestyle having to do with ritual. Yet I also had a deep sense of remorse for some of the things I heard, especially on the topic of Jesus. I think, though, that the "Jesus issue" is not an unbridgeable chasm for Jewish-Christian relations. I believe that Alan is saying that this world is worth our collective redemptive efforts, even for a short time. This is a thought I like.

Though our ways part on several theological and eschatological matters, and salvation looks quite different to each of us, I still sort of felt like Peter, James, and John on the Mount of Transfiguration watching Jesus in the company of Moses and Elijah. I wanted to learn more—to talk and listen more to Alan—and not leave Starbucks. This was a good feeling. When our visit was over, I was left hearing the whisper of God in my heart. I believe he was giving us his benediction.

three Listening to a Mormon

John R. Conlon

Samuel,* a leader in the Church of Jesus Christ of Latter-day Saints (LDS), confessed that his father swore he would never join the LDS religion. Samuel himself attended a nondenominational Christian church while an undergraduate student. What brought this friendly, soft-spoken professional to affirm the LDS faith is more a story of divine revelation than cognitive investigation.

Today, Samuel, a prominent physician in the community where he resides, is president of an LDS stake.† Samuel is a man exhibiting deep commitment to the principles of living taught by both LDS and Christian scripture. Following the interview, Samuel said, "I am not an official spokesman for the church. Much of what you asked me is church doctrine; the church is the source [that] should be used when [explaining its] doctrines . . . to others. Perhaps it would also be better if you referred to me as a local church leader, rather than by my name."

---

*Assumed name

†A "stake" is a jurisdictional area consisting of several wards (Mormon congregations).

JOHN: What is the most important thing in your life as a member of the LDS community?

SAMUEL [*without hesitation*]: The most important thing in my life is the knowledge that Jesus Christ is the Son of God, that he is the Savior and Redeemer of the world. He is my personal Savior. Our purpose in life is to worship God, to follow him, and to try to become like him. The standard for guiding our lives is the example that Jesus set when he lived on this earth. Though we often fall short, we are trying to be obedient to his example.

> Author's Note: In a booklet titled The Purpose of Life *the LDS church advises that "our Heavenly Father has a plan for individuals and families to find lasting peace and happiness. Through the teachings of His Son, the Lord Jesus Christ, through the scriptures and the words of modern prophets, and through the ordinances of His gospel, we can learn the purpose of our lives."*[1]

JOHN: What do you believe about God, human freedom, the natural world, and human relationships?

SAMUEL: We believe that Jesus Christ was born into mortality and lived on the earth. He preached his gospel, ministered to those around him, and ultimately atoned for the sins of all humankind. Following his crucifixion and resurrection, the church was guided by the apostles who spread the true gospel. Over time, many of the truths of the gospel that Jesus taught were lost, and the apostasy foretold by Paul occurred. Those conditions remained for nearly fifteen hundred years.

> Author's Note: LDS church doctrine as recorded by Bruce R. McConkie describes the apostasy thus: "This universal apostasy began in the days of the ancient apostles themselves (2 Pet. 2:1-

2); . . . Our Lord foretold the perplexities, calamities, and apostate wickedness of these same days. (Matt. 24; Mark 13; Luke 21.)"[2]

SAMUEL [*explaining further*]: After the death of those apostles, many false teachers brought division among the churches. By the time of Constantine the church was divided among many conflicting teachings all insisting their [doctrines were] right. The emperor brought church leaders together in council. Constantine's interest was in obtaining unity throughout the empire and not in correcting errors in church doctrine.

In the early nineteenth century a man named Joseph Smith was born into a religious family, some of whom had joined one church and some another. When Joseph was fourteen years of age, he was struggling to determine which church to join. He read in James, "If any of you lack wisdom, let him ask of God, that giveth to all men liberally, and upbraideth not" [1:5, KJV]. Joseph asked with a sincere heart, and in answer to his prayer, both God the Father and the Savior, Jesus Christ, visited him. He was told he should join none of [the churches], that the fullness of the gospel was soon to be restored to the earth. He learned from that experience that God is a glorified, resurrected being. His Son is also a glorified, resurrected being in "the express image of God." Joseph learned that we are literally created in the image of God and that he knows us and that the heavens are not closed. Those of the first-century church were called saints in the New Testament. Mormons are called Latter-day Saints today because the true gospel was restored to Joseph Smith in the latter days.

"We believe that men will be punished for their own sins, and not for Adam's transgression."[3] Although we inherit mortality from Adam, we are not responsible for his transgression. We are conceived and born into this world innocent. We are free to make choices throughout our entire lives. We access our freedom of choice by study, prayer, and personal worship. Worship is acknowledging Jesus to be the firstborn Son of Heavenly Father [and] then following all that he has instructed us to do. The gospel that Jesus taught is one of becoming. This life is a testing ground. It is a lifelong process of learning and becoming. Our test is to determine how we respond and treat others. The way we conduct ourselves as we grow and mature in this life determines our relationship with God.

JOHN: Why do you believe the way you do?

SAMUEL: In the *Book of Mormon* we read, "If ye shall ask with a sincere heart, with real intent, having faith in Christ, he will manifest the truth of it unto you, by the power of the Holy Ghost."[4] Each person, including you and me, may receive personal revelation from God. Through the witness of the Holy Ghost, I know that God lives, that Jesus is the Christ, and that fullness of the gospel has been restored to the earth with the keys and authority to preach the gospel and administer the ordinances of the gospel.

Author's Note: Gordon B. Hinckley, fifteenth president of the LDS church, described the person of God as understood by those of the LDS faith when writing the following: "Primary among Mormon teaching is belief and faith in God the Father, in Jesus Christ his Son, and in the Holy Ghost. But the Mormon concept is not set forth in vague creeds. It is simple and straightforward. God is in form like a man. . . . Jesus Christ is his Son, begotten in the flesh. . . . The Holy Ghost is a personage of spirit, yet nonetheless an individual personality. . . . These three distinct beings constitute the Godhead. The doctrine is explicit. It came about as a result of a remarkable experience: God the Father and Jesus Christ revealed themselves to Joseph Smith in answer to his prayer."[5]

In the Old Testament book of Exodus it is written that Moses talked with God face-to-face. Today God continues to reveal himself to his faithful. We believe that Jesus was the Jehovah of the Old Testament. God's communicating to human beings is a personal revelation to each person. It is tangible, but I find it impossible to explain in words.

Author's Note: There are two references in Exod. 33 to Moses' encounter with God: "And it came to pass, as Moses entered into the tabernacle, the cloudy pillar descended, and stood at the door of the tabernacle, and the LORD talked with Moses" (v. 9, KJV). "And it shall come to pass, while my glory passeth by, that I will put thee in a clift of the rock, and will cover thee with my hand while I pass by: And I will take away mine hand, and thou shalt see my back parts: but my face shall not be seen" (vv. 22-23, KJV).

JOHN: What do you believe about an afterlife?

SAMUEL: When we die, we are still alive. Each person has both a spirit and a body. Before this mortal life, we were born as the spirit children of our Father in heaven. He is literally our Father. When we are born here, our spirits are joined to a physical body. It is the natural order for us as children of a Heavenly Father.

Author's Note: The birth of spirit children is explained by McConkie thus: "Speaking of this prior existence in a spirit sphere, the First Presidency of the Church (Joseph F. Smith, John R. Winder, and Anthon H. Lund) said: 'All men and women are in the similitude of the universal Father and Mother, and are literally the sons and *daughters of Deity'; as spirits they were the 'offspring of celestial parentage. (*Man: His Origin and Destiny, *pp. 351, 355.)"[6]*

Eventually our bodies age and die, but the spirit continues to live while waiting for the resurrection when the spirit and body will again be joined together forever. It is a conscious waiting. Our spirit is a living thing. You've heard stories of people who have returned to a mortal life following an afterlife experience. They return from the dead to tell us that they recognized their loved ones who had gone on before. Those awaiting resurrection are recognizable, they have personalities, and they look like themselves. At the appointed time all will be resurrected. We will have bodies and live on in immortality. Some church leaders have said they believe we may be surprised at who all will be in heaven.

Author's Note: The LDS belief about heaven is summarized by Bruce McConkie, writing that the "highest among the kingdoms of glory hereafter is the celestial kingdom. . . . 'In the celestial glory *there are three heavens or degrees,' and in the same sense that baptism starts a person out toward an entrance into the celestial world, so celestial marriage puts a couple on the path leading to an exaltation in the highest heaven of that world. (D. & C. 131:1-4; 132.)"[7]*

JOHN: You have already made it clear that your choices in life lead to a destiny that is eternal. How do you attain that destiny?

SAMUEL: We understand that the atonement of Jesus Christ is infinite in nature. [*Samuel opened the* Book of Mormon *and read from 2 Nephi 25:23.*] In the *Book of Mormon* we read, "For we labor diligently to write, to persuade our children, and also our brethren, to believe in Christ, and to be reconciled to God; for we know that it is by grace that we are saved, after all we can do."[8] God asks us to do everything that we can, our very best effort, to repent and live the gospel and try to become like him. We also believe that there are ordinances that we must accomplish in mortality. The Savior said to Nicodemus, "Except a man be born of water and of the Spirit, he cannot enter into the kingdom of God" (John 3:5, KJV).

Our relationship is one of grace. Grace is a gift from God. We are taught to repent, and when we do, forgiveness is a gift. The requirements that God places on us are in accordance with our ability. We do not earn grace; it is a gift.

JOHN: Is the word "merit" more appropriate than "works"?

SAMUEL: We believe that we will be judged according to our works and the desires of our hearts. We are a covenant-making people. Covenant is a two-way agreement—an agreement in which God promises to do certain things and we promise to do certain things. What happens to us depends on how hard we are trying to keep the promises we have made to God. Again, "it is by grace that we are saved, after all we can do."

The gift of grace is not understood like some church groups who believe they are saved simply by saying they believe in Jesus then go about life any way they want. The one making a covenant with God also promises certain things. The ordinances include baptism and priesthood for all men. Temple ordinances such as endowment and sealing are also associated with covenants that we make with God. We are a covenant people. Making a covenant is making a promise.

Author's Note: LDS doctrine defines sealing to be "Those ordinances performed in the temples whereby husbands and wives are sealed together in the marriage union for time and eternity, and whereby children are sealed eternally to parents."[9]

JOHN: What principles or rules, if any, do you think are basic to living?

SAMUEL: Living a Christlike life is basic to our faith. "If there is anything virtuous, lovely, or of good report or praiseworthy, we seek after these things."[10] John Wentworth, an editor of the *Chicago Democrat* newspaper, asked Joseph Smith to summarize the history of the church and its doctrines. At the end of his response he wrote thirteen statements of church doctrine. These thirteen statements have come to be accepted as the Articles of Faith of the Church of Jesus Christ of Latter-day Saints.

The Articles of Faith as Originally Written by Joseph Smith

1. We believe in God, the Eternal Father, and in His Son, Jesus Christ, and in the Holy Ghost.
2. We believe that men will be punished for their own sins, and not for Adam's transgression.
3. We believe that through the Atonement of Christ, all mankind may be saved, by obedience to the laws and ordinances of the Gospel.
4. We believe that the first principles and ordinances of the Gospel are: first, Faith in the Lord Jesus Christ; second, Repentance; third, Baptism by immersion for the remission of sins; fourth, Laying on of hands for the gift of the Holy Ghost.
5. We believe that a man must be called of God, by prophecy, and by the laying on of hands by those who are in authority, to preach the Gospel and administer in the ordinances thereof.
6. We believe in the same organization that existed in the Primitive Church, namely, apostles, prophets, pastors, teachers, evangelists, and so forth.
7. We believe in the gift of tongues, prophecy, revelation, visions, healing, interpretation of tongues, and so forth.
8. We believe the Bible to be the word of God as far as it is translated correctly; we also believe the Book of Mormon to be the word of God.

9. We believe all that God has revealed, all that He does now reveal, and we believe that He will yet reveal many great and important things pertaining to the Kingdom of God.

10. We believe in the literal gathering of Israel and in the restoration of the Ten Tribes; that Zion (the New Jerusalem) will be built upon the American continent; that Christ will reign personally upon the earth; and that the earth will be renewed and receive its paradisiacal glory.

11. We claim the privilege of worshiping Almighty God according to the dictates of our own conscience, and allow all men the same privilege, let them worship how, where, or what they may.

12. We believe in being subject to kings, presidents, rulers, and magistrates, in obeying, honoring, and sustaining the law.

13. We believe in being honest, true, chaste, benevolent, virtuous, and in doing good to all men; indeed, we may say that we follow the admonition of Paul—We believe all things, we hope all things, we have endured many things, and hope to be able to endure all things. If there is anything virtuous, lovely, or of good report or praiseworthy, we seek after these things.[11]

JOHN: How do you decide what is right or wrong in any situation?

SAMUEL: In the book of John it states, "In the beginning was the Word, and the Word was with God, and the Word was God. The same was in the beginning with God. All things were made by him; and without him was not any thing made that was made. In him was life; and the life was the light of men" [1:1-4, KJV]. Everyone has this "light of Christ." In the *Book of Mormon* we read, "For behold, the Spirit of Christ is given to every man that he may know good from evil; wherefore, I show unto you the way to judge; for every thing which inviteth to do good, and to persuade to believe in Christ, is sent forth by the power and gift of Christ; wherefore ye may know with a perfect knowledge it is of God."[12]

We could call this light our conscience. Everyone has it. It is a gift of the Holy Ghost. Everyone knows the difference between right and wrong. Even the most callous offender knows what he is doing and whether it is right or wrong. Even someone like Charles Manson must have had some knowledge that what he was doing was wrong when he committed murder. We each make our decisions based on what we want to do in this life. When we make wrong decisions, those decisions are made with the knowledge that they are wrong.

JOHN: Why do bad things happen to good people?

SAMUEL: Unhappy things occur as a condition of our mortality. This life is a time when we receive a physical body, but it is also a time of preparation. The *Book of Mormon* states, "For behold, this life is the time for men to prepare to meet God; yea, behold the day of this life is the day for men to perform their labors."[13] Our Father in heaven sees things from a different perspective than we do; his is an eternal perspective. We are stuck in a whisper of time in eternity, and we cannot see the big picture. Perhaps the difficult things that happen are challenges that help us to prepare for a future that waits beyond this mortal existence. In order to mature we require challenges.

JOHN: What do you think about the idea of checks and balances in the universe (i.e., a final judgment or karma)?

SAMUEL: The Heavenly Father is a God of law. The person most obedient to that law was Christ. The stars, the universe, everything—is governed by the laws put in place by God the Father. The natural order of things is subject to the laws instituted by God. He is perfectly just; but he is also perfectly merciful. What happens is not by chance, but it all depends on law and how hard we are trying.

JOHN: How does mainstream Christianity compare with the LDS belief?

SAMUEL: We believe in God, the Eternal Father, and in his Son, Jesus Christ, and in the Holy Ghost. We believe that Heavenly Father and his Son and the Holy Ghost are separate beings who are one in purpose and intent. The Father and the Son are glorified, resurrected beings; the Holy Ghost is a personage of spirit. They are eternal, omnipotent, and omniscient. The *Doctrine and Covenants* speaks of the Savior: "He comprehendeth all things, and all things are before him, and all things are round about him; and he is above all things, and in all things, and is through all things, and is round about all things; and all things are by him, and of him, even God, forever and ever."[14] Both Heavenly Father and the Son, Jesus Christ, exist [each] in a body that is in one place. It is their influence that is omnipresent. It is their influence that is everywhere at all times.

We believe in a premortal existence where we are all born as spirit children—the sons and daughters of Heavenly Father. We are created in his image. Mortality opens the way for spirit-born sons and daughters to progress as Heavenly Father did in a world before our time. I don't know how all that came about. I cannot understand a doctrine of [the] Trinity nor do I find it explained in the Bible.

Author's Note: In his doctrinal interpretation of the LDS concept of spirit, McConkie concludes that "This spirit element has always existed; it is co-eternal with God. (Teachings, pp. 352-354.) . . . Speaking of pre-existent spirits, Abraham calls them 'The intelligences that were organized before the world was.' (Abra. 3:22-24.) Thus, portions of the self-existent spirit element are born as spirit children, or in other words, the intelligence which cannot be created or made, because it is self-existent, is organized into intelligences."[15]

JOHN: What do you think about mainstream Christianity?

SAMUEL: All the Christian denominations are great. And all Christians are wonderful. We respect and admire the other Christian religions. We are all trying to live good lives and follow the Savior. When you compare us with mainstream Christianity, we have a few more pieces to the eternal picture than they, but we are all sons and daughters of God.

JOHN: How do your beliefs influence your daily life and your relationships with others?

SAMUEL: Our first priority is to follow the teachings of Jesus Christ. Our responsibility is to be honest [and] ethical and in every way [to] offer a helping hand to those about us. Scripture tells us to live in the world but not to be worldly in our attitudes and deeds. We should be temperate in all our relationships; in all of our involvement with other persons we are admonished to stay on a moral path. This gospel of Jesus Christ compels us to do our best work in whatever circumstances we find ourselves.

Author's Note: My conversation with Samuel concluded soon after he made these important comments. What he said about the way Latter-day Saints reach out and help others is true. I've experienced it firsthand. My wife and I lived in the city of Orem, Utah, where I was employed as the pastor of the New Beginnings Fellowship Church of the Nazarene in Provo, Utah. We lived there for seven years. Throughout that time men from the local LDS ward*

---

*A "ward" is a Mormon congregation.

would come to our house and shovel snow during blizzards. The ward bishop made a point to help in any time of need. On one occasion I was hospitalized with pneumonia. While I was in the hospital, a neighbor mowed my lawn twice. Another neighbor brought cooked food to my wife more than once. Another neighbor brought her class of young people to the hospital to wish me well. Then when we moved away, three neighbors, knowing that we would never return and that we were not LDS members, came and thoroughly cleaned our house. These were acts of neighborly koinōnia, to put it into book of Acts terms, and lessons about treating others that all people can learn from, especially those of us who call ourselves part of Christianity's mainstream.

Listening to a Secular Humanist
My Friend Jim

Jim Wicks

The thought of "interviewing" my friend Jim for a book made me nervous. I didn't want him to feel I was exploiting our friendship. But as we sat talking at the kitchen table about the need for new paradigms, our philosophical differences were absorbed into the warmth of our goodwill toward each other. That day I began a conversation that would prove to be one of the most thought-provoking discussions I ever had. As a secular humanist, Jim could find an explanation for the world without appealing to the divine. For me, the world pointed us to the divine. Surprisingly, in this discussion and in others we've had throughout our friendship, we explored our differences and discovered more in common than either of us could have imagined.

As I prepared for the interview, I reflected back to when I first met Jim. Two years earlier, my wife, Gina, and I were downtown at the famous Portland Saturday Market with our two boys, Jake and Jeremiah, searching for a place to eat lunch. After settling on where and what to eat, we began looking for a spot where all four of us could sit. Now this task was more challenging than it might sound because my oldest son was in a wheelchair. I remember the pressure I felt on that hot summer's day. The crowd was busy, the music was loud, and we were all tired from trying to juggle plates of heaping noodles purchased from one of the many street vendors.

As sweat rose on my forehead, I heard a faint voice floating through the crowd, "Hey! Jim Wicks, is that you?" Shocked to see Jamie, a former student of ours, I almost dropped my plate, noodles and all. I had heard she recently moved to the Portland area after finishing her nursing degree and getting married. Today she was with a tall, good-looking young man that I quickly deduced must be her husband. Standing in that crowded market, we were able to reconnect with this young lady who had been close to our family so many years ago. Jamie was in our youth group when she was in high school, but she had also later lived with us for one summer. Clearly I would be understating if I said we were not overjoyed to see her.

That fall Jamie began attending our church, and as we got reacquainted with her, I began to understand the joyful feelings I felt that day at the market. In our relationship with Jamie and her husband, Jim, a deeper story began to develop—a story that goes beyond family, school, career, and even Jamie. Yet all of these areas of life are also interconnected, interdependent, and part of the story. That is to say, being with this great couple over the last couple of years and understanding what an integral part they play in our lives has been fulfilling.

On one occasion Jamie and Jim ministered to my family in such a way that I have a hard time finding words to express how it affected me. Our son Jacob needed several major operations last year because he was born with spina bifida, which is a neural-tube defect[1] that has left him with a host of complex health issues over the course of his short fifteen years of life. Jamie had always loved Jacob like a little brother and even in high school showed her empathy for our family and special love for him. But now I found that Jim, who had a career doing research work in neuroscience, was also sitting with us in the hospital waiting room while Jacob endured twelve hours of surgery. During that time Jim shared that he had also suffered several childhood ailments, and now well-equipped in his understanding of the developmental process and science of the human brain, he expressed a deep compassion for Jacob.

Both Jamie and Jim came into the intensive care unit immediately after surgery to see our son, who was still a bit loopy from anesthesia and pain medication. Jacob was inviting all his visitors to check out the results of his operation. Jim, who had endured several major childhood surgeries, found everything a little overwhelming and had to dismiss himself. I think in hindsight he just wanted to give our family some privacy. Not surprisingly, as an operating room nurse, Jamie loved every minute of it.

During the next several weeks that we were in the hospital, Jim and Jamie were faithful almost every day to come and check on Jake and the whole family. One day when our youngest son became bored and was wandering the halls playing with some of the other children who were recovering, Jim took him to his lab. For Jeremiah the experience was amazing: lab rats, mice, microscopes, lab coats, big black glasses, and so on. For me this occasion brought back memories of my own youth when my interests were piqued as I listened to my dad teach high school biology. Jeremiah was like a kid in a candy store, and I appreciated Jim's heart and the love he demonstrated for my family.

Jim also displays his heart for people in his home. I love when he decides to cook a meal. He once prepared a huge dinner for a party celebrating Jamie's graduation from a master's program. He went all out, making sure to prepare so much food that no guest could leave without a chance of getting full. He even cooked Jamie's grandpa's favorite cut of beef, which meant a lot to that retired cattle rancher. He approached the whole thing like a huge experiment, graciously but firmly intervening when Jamie kept opening the oven. Instructing her to close it, he worried over the meat cooking inside as if it were an eighth grade chemistry project that had to come to a boil at just the right time. Jamie, on the other hand, behaved like an operating room nurse. When the meat was ready, she handed Jim the knife he requested as if it were a scalpel and the beef were a patient awaiting the first incision. Watching the entire thing, I almost cracked up laughing.

Needless to say my family and I love this couple, and I am thankful to call Jim and Jamie my friends. As our story with them unfolds, we are discovering that our lives are even more connected than we expected. One day we realized that Jim's father lives in the same town where I grew up in north central Idaho. I even graduated from high school with his stepsister. I also enjoy sharing adventure stories with Jim, who, like me, has a fondness for the outdoors, reading, philosophy, and coffee. We like to chat about renewable energy, transportation, new political paradigms, and our favorite topic—health care reform.

Jim, who holds a Ph.D. in neuroscience, performs research that investigates the complexities of the brain. His goal is to discover new truths that may lead us to a more complete understanding of the human mind and its role in illness and health. The work fascinates me, and Jim is eager to break down the ideas to fit my limited understanding so that he can share with me the complexities of scientific exploration. For me this interaction with Jim is not only beautiful but also transforming and redemptive. I don't feel this way because of the information that is exchanged but because I enjoy the idea that two men from different generations and backgrounds can sit down and share a common passion for helping people. The Jim I have come to know is just as committed as I am to pursuing truths that we can share.

An important conversation that Jim and I approach with much contemplation and sensitivity is that concerning spirituality and science. We come to it desiring it to be a conversation birthed out of relational connectivity and respect. We also realize that history has not shown the kindness deserved by the sensitivities of these two areas of discussion.

As the pastor of a young church I also pursue new truths, not through microscopes and statistics, but by engaging people on a spiritual level. From this, I constantly encounter people hurt by the church or who disregard it. I believe that in many ways we live in a post-Christian, postchurch environment. The church is preoccupied with clarifying the orthodoxy and orthopraxis of rhetoric and reform and whether the word "emerging" presents a challenge to the heritage of Christianity. All the while the world continues to self-actualize and identify the church as nonconversant with important issues. In many ways, the world has moved on as we, the church, continue to be stymied by age-old discussions. In my experience, the church often lacks engagement at all levels, and we have lost the art of reflection and relevancy in most situations.

I have my own opinions about these struggles between the world and the church and may someday say more about them—but not now. Instead I want you to listen to a friend of mine share his curiosity about why so many Christians cannot see another side of the truth they speak of so definitively. The kind of truth he knows about can be defended on the basis of sound scientific method and reason, and it can be reproduced.

In this conversation, listening to the voice of my friend Jim is important because he has found another way to reason through the questions of this naturally mysterious world. To be sure, I have no desire whatsoever to "conquer" Jim, nor do I believe that such a goal is necessary or achievable. I do, however, want to emphasize to the reader the inexpressible respect I have for this young man. So let's sit back and listen to a scientist's understanding of a good way to interpret life.

Questions About Belief System and Worldview

JW: What is the most important thing in your life as a secular humanist?

JIM: I usually don't classify myself as anything in particular, but it is more or less the train of thought that I fall into. Secular humanism would be more of a proactive viewpoint by default.

JW: What is the purpose of life?

JIM: Family.

JW: What shaped that?

JIM: [I] never really discussed it as a family, but growing up with a single mom, family became central as an unconditional safe environment. [We] had to be there for each other. [I] never really understood "tough love." You don't give up on family no matter how bad they screw up. Friends are also important.

JW: How do you define meaningful relationships?

JIM: It depends on the type of relationship. . . . Friendships have different criteria: [You] feel close, appreciate who they are, [and so on]. I don't feel I need to have the same kind of relationship with everyone I work or play with. [For] example: [I have] close friends from high school [that I] only see once or twice a year versus work relations that I see every day but don't consider close. . . . In family, my role has been the "stable" one or the "fixer." [I had] a lot of animosity with [my] brother because I took on the role of father figure.

JW: What were the contributing factors from your family that influenced your worldview?

JIM: They played a strong role in how I behave practically—hardworking, caring, [kind], [and so on]—but not so much in how I think about the world. Regarding religion, I navigated religiosity on my own and came to my own conclusions, [which] are different [from those of] my parents and brother, [and this] sometimes is contentious.

JW: At what point did you diverge from your family on religious beliefs?

JIM: We never really talked about things like religion, sex, [and] college explicitly in my home growing up. My mom chose to model how to behave more than verbally telling us what to do, so there really was nothing to depart from. I took it upon myself to start going to church around [age] eleven or twelve, and I started to form my own opinions about that because [there was never much of a] formalized point of view in my house. I don't know what my mom's beliefs are in particular, but I know that a higher power has a role in her life because I think she needs that. But if you came over to our house, we wouldn't talk about religion in three months. I think my mom models quite well a [broad] respect . . . for a lot of different viewpoints and religions. With my dad, we have a lot of ideas in common, but [we] come to very different conclusions. . . .

. . . I remember [going] to a friend's funeral in seventh grade. They gave an altar call at the funeral, and I think now that [that] borders on exploitation, and it scared . . . me, even then. Young children are unaware of religious affiliation when they are making friends. But early on, kids would come to school just repeating what they had heard at home about politics and religion, and I remember being very confused about what they were talking about and why. All I knew is that we didn't go to their church, so we must [have embodied] the bad things they were talking about. I don't think children should have to shoulder that burden and worry about those things.

JW: How do you think the story would be different if those experiences would have been more positive?

JIM: For every one of those negative experiences, there were also a lot of positive ones, too, so I don't know if there would be that much difference. But childhood experiences [carry] a lot of weight in your memory and are very formative. It's hard to speculate, but I imagine that could have made a difference. For me, those are definitely a component of my understanding, but they are not the reason . . . I came to the conclusions . . . I did about God.

JW: Why are we here?

JIM: I don't think there is a codified universal purpose for life given by a supernatural power. In a biological sense, I think there are reasons we do things. As humans I think we have the ability to be responsible and create that purpose ourselves. I don't feel that my life is meaningless without belief in a higher power. There are some really universal things that I think should be human priorities, but [they are] not due to some underlying cosmic power. If we were to talk about what I feel my purpose is, [I'd say] be a responsible citizen, do good work, enjoy life, be present in life, give back to the community, and love family and friends. I think those are all universally important. But my social priorities (care about people and do good) are different from my work priorities (to discover new things), and I don't feel a drive to invoke a universal power that joins all aspects of my life.

JW: What if one person's purpose is to wreak havoc?

JIM: That falls under the realm of ethics and morals in my mind, and there is arguably a moral difference between the purpose of doing good and killing people. People from all different positions will agree that murder is wrong, not just because it is against the law. I don't think we behave [most of the time] because we are afraid to break the law, but these are fundamental philosophical questions. And I don't think we inherently need religion to help us answer these questions.

JW: Where do these desires come from? What is it about humanity that knows the difference between right and wrong?

JIM: I think the framework [for] that is genetically derived because [it has] evolved over time as social adaptations to survival, a product of our natural development that promotes fecundity. . . . these good behaviors are actually biologically important behaviors for the survival of society (natural selection). In a very true sense, there is not really any way to prove that there is not a God factor, but [it] is not the most reasonable explanation, so why would you invoke a higher power if you can't prove it. [Yet] you do know . . . other factors to be true. For example, if you believe that God is loving and altruistic . . . and that God is in control of everything, then you end up with a lot of questions about why certain things happen. . . . [A belief in a loving God in control of everything is] hard to reconcile with a world of suffering. So the more likely answer in my mind is that we are a product of the natural world and sometimes it appears fair and sometimes it doesn't, and that is all a part of the natural order of things.

JW: How do you worship? What does worship mean to you?

JIM: I think the closest thing I do to worship is being outside in nature when I am able to appreciate the natural world and be a part of that. I appreciate the power of the natural world and am perplexed and amazed at how it works and that it goes on whether or not I am there. Maybe visiting my family is a form of worship. I think of worship as a form of submission and acknowledgment.

JW: What do you believe about God, human freedom, the natural world, human relationships?

JIM: I don't believe in God or gods or the supernatural. I don't like to use the word "believe" because it means to me that I am doing [something] without reason or evidence. [I'd rather] say that I know some things and I don't know some things. But belief to me is an opinion about something in lieu of evidence. [Usually] in the scientific world we are left with choosing the most likely answer based on the best evidence, which is subject to change. [The] litmus for truth in science [means something must be] internally consistent, externally consistent, . . . explainable (not supernaturally invoked [from outside] the realm of science), . . . predictive, . . . parsimonious (Occam's razor: the simplest answer is the most probable). But I also do not judge everything using scientific principles. Art, for example, does not need to pass these tests to be valid. But many people who claim to have faith will not change their beliefs/viewpoints if they are challenged by truth, and I don't live my life like that. I feel drawn to satirical stories, like Mark Twain's *Diaries of Adam and Eve*, that speak of the human nature and doing things because we are curious and not necessarily out of disobedience.

JW: Why do you believe the way you do?

JIM: On a religious level there are two parts to that answer: (1) Technical reasons [for] why I don't believe in God are the lack of evidence in the natural world; [there are no] compelling . . . reasons for me to know God exists. (2) I don't practice in a religious community, because there are behaviors that come out of religious systems that are troubling to me, and I don't want to be involved in [them].

JW: What do you believe about an afterlife? What happens when you die?

JIM: I don't. When you die, the best I can guess is that it's like passing out and you are no longer cognizant. It's hard to know what exactly happens; it seems [as though] we like to try to explain our experiences. There are some scientific theories about the "white light" that people see, but we really don't know what is going on; it's a mystery. Mystery is not incompatible with science.

JW: Why can't we become comfortable with mystery?

JIM: I think that to navigate the world, we construct explanations about things that we don't understand. I think that this is really self-limiting. I am forced to conclude that many people with religious beliefs are arrogant or ignorant and very uncreative because they have the "answer" to everything, and it is embodied in a very narrow, strange political figure. I think this is a very self-serving attitude that keeps God on your side.

Questions About Lifestyle

JW: How do your beliefs influence your daily life?

JIM: I think the present is very important because that is all we have. I try to step back and [hold] a bigger picture approach and keep [my] perspective on the brevity of life.

JW: At the end of your time on earth, how would you want to be remembered?

JIM: My work is really important to me right now, but I am positive that having my family taken care of is much more important to me. [I want to] raise good children and hopefully leave the world a little bit better.

Questions About Ethics

JW: How do your beliefs affect your relationships with others?

JIM: Maybe on a more global scale the idea of social justice and basic human rights plays a major role in guiding my decisions about what is right or wrong and how people should be treated. I think about what constitutes a basic human right and what we are entitled to just because we are born into the world. At a minimum I think this should include food, shelter, access to health care, and education. This idea that people [who] have less . . . are somehow milking the system is not a judgment that I want to make. Thinking about how people interact, I often [consider] the nature of the relationship. . . . the distribution of power is really important to me, especially when people with the power exploit a relationship [they have] with someone less fortunate. That is my framework that I try to live by.

JW: What ethical principles do you live by?

JIM: I believe in justice and fairness but not retribution, because I think those are different things. I think just laws are important for a society, but [we must also] include the principles of caring for others [because] we don't make progress as a society unless we are all moving forward together and not leaving some behind. I try to avoid materialism as much as possible.

JW: What effect do your choices have on your destiny?

JIM: We are a product of our choices. I mean, there are a lot of things we can't choose, but I think choices are very critical to where we end up. However, I also think [that] the starting point is very relevant and we have to take that into consideration and that money is central to that starting point.

JW: What principles or rules, if any, do you think are basic to living?

JIM: You have to be patient. Loving your family; being a good friend. Integrity and honesty.

JW: How do you decide what is right or wrong in any situation?

JIM: I decide based on the information I have access to, and I hold this up against my internal measures for right and wrong, but I have to consider the situation. I think there are a few things that are wrong no matter what, but I am more relativistic in other areas. I try to reserve passing judgment unless it's germane to me or [if] I think it will hurt or negatively affect someone else. I definitely think our choices profoundly affect others.

JW: Where do you draw the line when making choices involving others?

JIM: It depends on who the others are. . . . People [whom] I feel comfortable with I am more likely to give . . . my opinion. I don't expect . . . everyone [to have] the same set of standards as [me], but at the same time I do interact with my family and try to help form their behaviors in a way that seems healthy to me. I try to be aware of social situations by reminding myself that I should be the one to act if I see someone that needs help, because often people in groups can walk by and I don't want to [do the same and just] expect someone else to do something about it.

JW: Why do bad things happen to good people?

JIM: I think bad things just happen. I don't think you will get clean answers on that, like why do good things happen to bad people?

JW: What do you think about the idea of checks and balances in the universe?

JIM: It works great when things work out, but bad things happen to everyone and this argument seems to fall apart pretty quickly in the face of reality, and then you have to find reasons why these bad things happen—and I just don't believe that bad things happen for a reason. Absolutely nothing would bring me comfort in a horrible situation that had no fairness (e.g., children's suffering and death).

Questions About Christianity

JW: What do you think Christians believe?

JIM: Fundamentally, I think it boils down to a belief that humans are inherently fallen and not complete and that you must believe in Christ as the Son of God to find that completeness. From there it breaks off into many different permutations. If I were to donate money, I would rather give to an organization that is not affiliated with a religion because I think you should do good things because it is the correct thing to do, not because of an agenda.

JW: What experiences have you had with Christians?

JIM: All kinds; you find all sorts of people involved in Christianity, and I have decided you can't judge [persons] by their religious or political affiliations. My assumption from experience and literature is that the vast majority of people in the world believe in God, so I am different from the vast majority. Usually that doesn't bother me, but there are times when I cannot tolerate certain evangelical behaviors. [For] example, Christian extremists on [a university] campus yelling hate. I always wonder, what is the goal of evangelical behaviors? If it really is to make the world a better place, would your time be better spent working indirectly behind the scenes to feed and clothe the poor, eradicate poverty, and so on? Or do you need the public affirmation? I think that sometimes what it comes down to for Christians is explaining everything within a Christian framework, which sounds to the outsider like, "My beliefs are correct, and yours are wrong or not valid."

JW: How does Christianity compare with what you believe?

JIM: If it stands for social justice, then I stand with it, but if it stands for judgment and eternal damnation, then I stand opposed to it. So I guess it depends on your definition of Christianity. But I don't hold the central tenet that humans are fundamentally wanting and that they are in need of salvation from a god.

JW: What do think about Christianity?

JIM: It's complex. I respect it primarily because I know people to whom it is very important, and I can respect it for the greatness that comes out of it. But I am completely ready to hold the church responsible for the full weight of its bad characteristics.

JW: What do you think about Christians?

JIM: I think there are a lot . . . of varieties. I don't think just because [some persons] say they are Christians, they are inherently better or worse than anyone else. I am probably going to have some preconceived notions about what they believe, but I will not withhold friendship from someone based on [his or her] religious beliefs.

JW: What do you think about Jesus and his teachings?

JIM: I think the words written for Jesus are good philosophies, but I don't think Jesus originated a lot of the philosophies in the Bible. I think a lot of these ideas were already out there, so I don't attribute much novel work to him. But on the whole I do think Jesus was a good teacher and philosopher. I am not convinced about whether Jesus was a literal or figurative person in history.

o o o

Our interview came to a close, and I was more than grateful to Jim for allowing me to ask him several hours of questions, some of which many Christians would never attempt to answer. I once tried to ask a fellow believer about such matters, and he said those things were between him and God alone; they were just too personal to discuss. But for Jim, who doesn't believe in God, answering such questions would not be anything personal, just reasonable. Maybe that's an approach we should all consider, especially when talking to others who believe or think differently from us.

five Listening to Scientologists

Michael Vasquez

(Editor's Note: Knowing from experience the difficulty of dialoging with Scientologists about their belief system, Michael Vasquez does not approach his topic through a one-on-one interview. His impressions are instead personal and shaped from years living in an area regularly exposed to Scientology's influences.)

I have lived in Hollywood for the past twenty years or so. Every day I drive past at least one of the many Scientology centers in Hollywood. The center I pass the most is the world headquarters of the Church of Scientology, a big blue building that was once a Christian hospital. It has a cross on top of it, but now as a Scientology training center there is nothing Christian about it.

When I bring up the subject of Scientology to the people in my church, audible groans are often heard. Most, if not all, have had dealings with the "church." It is not easy to avoid Scientology on the streets of Hollywood. Walking on Hollywood Boulevard you are almost certain to pass one of the centers, and when you do, you're greeted by a representative of the church who politely asks if you'd like to take a free personality test. I personally have taken the test a number of times, and each time is pretty much the same. First you take the written portion of the test, and then you are shown the many areas of your life that the Church of Scientology can assist you in correcting. Although this seems like just another self-help course, it is very different. The Church of Scientology vehemently renounces psychology and believes that only their practices can free you. You are next shown a movie that describes what Scientology is about, and then you're subjected to a hard sell on their materials, their philosophy, and their science and religion. Hollywood is one of the world capitals for Scientology.

When you walk by the Scientology center on Sunset Boulevard in Hollywood, you will notice many of the practitioners dressed in attire similar to what Scientology's founder, L. Ron Hubbard, wore when he was in the navy. Those who wear this naval attire are members of the Sea Organization, an elite group of workers who have contracted themselves to serve Scientology "for a billion years."[1] The street on which the center is located was renamed after Hubbard. Several times throughout the year the main parking lot in front of the building is closed off and large tents are erected for people coming together from throughout the world to meet and celebrate Scientology. These are often closed meetings, with the presence of security evident to any outsiders trying to get in.

Part of the reason Scientology is so successful in Los Angeles and especially in Hollywood is that so many people have flocked to this area to rebuild their lives. They want to piece together their shattered dreams and make new names for themselves. But many of them have found nothing but more heartache, more pain, and more disillusionment, and they find themselves looking for someone who can give them direction and hope. The Church of Scientology sees this and pretends to offer solutions to these many shattered lives. It promises to give them back clear minds and hearts. To do so, each person must clear away everything that stands in the way of a personal spirit—a being called a thetan— who has lived many lifetimes and now lives inside the person. A person's thetan must be cleansed of the things of this world so that, as Scientologists explain, "You can be the complete you."

This cleansing or purification can take place in one of the Scientology centers, such as the purification center on Sunset Boulevard in Los Angeles. There a person is *audited*, that is, counseled and given additional tests, and as each test reveals the flaws in that person's personality or makeup, he or she is then offered many different teaching packages, most of which were compiled by L. Ron Hubbard. As a person grows deeper and deeper in the teachings, he or she invests hundreds, if not thousands, of dollars. Yet even after tens of thousands of dollars are exhausted, there's still more that must be purified from clients. When practitioners, disillusioned with the church's teachings and the vast amounts of money they invested, consider leaving the church, high pressure is applied to get them to stay. Once the church has a person willing to sign over his or her life savings, even his or her house and land, it doesn't let go easily.

I would often ask Scientology representatives about their founder's background and about the many magazine and newspaper articles written by families of loved ones who had lost great amounts of money to the church. There are also stories from people actually involved in Scientology who tried to leave, only to find their way barred. The representatives I spoke with denied all the allegations that were in print and generally gave me the company line. While I was writing this chapter, just a couple days ago a young man entered a worldwide center of Scientology in Hollywood, brandishing two samurai swords and vowing revenge for how Scientology messed up his life. The young man was shot to death by one of the guards in the Scientology Hospitality Center. Getting a clear, objective answer about the dealings of Scientology from a practitioner is difficult if not impossible.

Some Definitions

What follows are some basic definitions to help you understand more about Scientology's background and beliefs.

Church—The "Church of Scientology" is a relatively new term. The Scientology group may have sought the "church" designation to evade taxation. In 1967 the Internal Revenue Service "stripped Scientology's mother church of its tax-exempt status. A federal court ruled in 1971 that . . . [it] could no longer be called a scientific treatment" center.[2] Hubbard and the organization at this time sought full religious status, "seeking First Amendment protection for Scientology's" so-called church.[3]

Dianetics—The source literature and religious philosophy of founder L. Ron Hubbard, with amendments by his practitioners.

L. Ron Hubbard—The founder of the Church of Scientology was born on March 13, 1911. A science fiction writer initially, Hubbard pieced together a number of different philosophies to organize his system of ideas and techniques called Dianetics. "Hubbard served in the Navy during World War II" and was a somewhat successful writer of science fiction novels.[4] Official church literature "described him falsely as an 'extensively decorated' World War II hero who was crippled and blinded in action, twice pronounced dead and miraculously cured through Scientology. Hubbard's 'doctorate' from 'Sequoia University' was a fake mail-order degree."[5]

Scientology—The official position given by the church is that Scientology is a new religion and applied religious philosophy and that it reflects the ideals and philosophical practice of its founder, L. Ron Hubbard, and his belief that the spirit of man is the center of all that is wrong with man and in turn must be liberated.

Thetans—The term also used in the Church of Scientology is the word for the spiritual beings that reside in us. The word and definition changes are dependent on the literature you research, but the most common definitions describe thetans as beings beyond ourselves, contained within us, and in need of liberation so that we can be all that we were meant to be.

Celebrity Status

Scientology has long been known for the Hollywood celebrities it has attracted. Such big names as "Tom Cruise and John Travolta, actresses Kirstie Alley, Mimi Rogers, and Anne Archer, Palm Springs mayor and performer Sonny Bono, jazzman Chick Corea and even Nancy Cartwright, the voice of cartoon star Bart Simpson," are all associated with the Church of Scientology.[6]

The majority of Scientology practitioners, however, are not the rich and famous but desperate people looking for answers. "To pay their fees, newcomers can earn commissions by recruiting new members, become auditors themselves . . . or join the church staff and receive free counseling in exchange for what their written contracts describe as a 'billion years' of labor."[7]

As a pastor who has worked on the streets of Hollywood for the past twenty years, it breaks my heart to see the deception Scientology offers. I believe in Jesus Christ, and I believe he alone is my Savior. I know that his Holy Spirit resides within me and not the spirit of another being who has lived countless lives over and over again as Scientology teaches, a being who is seeking to be liberated from me so that it can rise to its own higher purpose. Seeing Jesus glorified is my highest aim.

How many times have we seen people turn to different teachings in this world, thinking that the truth is out there somewhere else when Jesus is right here offering us eternal life, a life in relationship with him? I'm reminded of how the Bible says that the thief comes "to steal, and to kill, and to destroy." Jesus says, "I have come that [you] may have life, and that [you] may have it more abundantly" (John 10:10, NKJV). When I see people who are poor of money, heart, and spirit walking through the doors of Scientology and giving what little they have, I want to tell them to turn around and come to Jesus and know that he has what they are looking for and will give it to them freely—that he truly can grant them the fulfillment they're seeking.

Listening to an Atheist/Agnostic
My Friend Ryan

Scott Daniels

For a minister to become friends with someone who professes to be an agnostic or an atheist is unusual. Most of the time the differences—both assumed and real—keep a genuine relationship from taking place between those who openly profess to be believers in Jesus Christ and those who profess unbelief.

What really brought Ryan and me together as friends was God's providence. I was a college professor for about ten years. During those years when a new acquaintance would ask me what I did for a living, even though I was also an ordained minister, I would say, "I'm an ethics professor." (I would leave out the "theological" adjective in "theological ethics.") That would usually lead to an interesting discussion no matter what the belief system of the other person. Now that I am a pastor and have no choice but to face up to my true vocation, conversations with nonbelievers are often pretty short.

But Ryan, in a way, sought me out. My first Sunday as pastor in Pasadena, California, Ryan caught me on the patio at church and introduced himself by saying, "My name is Ryan. You may see me at church from time to time because my wife is a believer, and I love her and try to be supportive of her. But I don't believe any of this stuff."

I was able to carry on the conversation long enough to discover that Ryan was a very well-respected literature teacher at a local high school. Ryan was certainly not attacking me or my belief system, but he wanted to be sure that I knew, from the very beginning of whatever relationship we were to have, several important things about him. He wanted me to know that he had reasoned through the philosophical issues about God and had reasonably decided that more than likely there is no God (atheism) and if by some remote chance there is a God, little if anything could be known about him, and he (she, they, or it) mattered little to everyday life (agnosticism).

What was incredibly refreshing about Ryan was that he was up front with his confidence in the intellectual superiority of a lack of belief. I sensed that he was willing to be my friend because he did not think I was ignorant. But it was clear that from his perspective at the time, faith is something people have when they haven't really thought through the crazy logic of their convictions. I don't believe he would have said that faith was for the weak, but he certainly didn't believe it was for the enlightened.

After that initial encounter I began to notice Ryan attending worship every Sunday for three or four months. Puzzled that he had a better attendance record than most people who do profess belief in Jesus, I caught him one week on the patio and said, "Hey, Ryan. It is good to see you. For someone who doesn't believe in any of this stuff, you are sure here a lot." He responded with my favorite compliment ever. He said, "You're right, Scott. I still don't believe anything. But I do find you very rhetorically pleasing."

I laughed hysterically and a true friendship began. I asked him what he liked to read, and we began reading books together. He bought me Dostoyevsky's *The Idiot* for us to read. I found it so fascinating that someone who so openly professed a lack of faith would be drawn to Dostoyevsky's novel about a Christ figure who lives in radical contrast to the values of the society around him.

We began a dialogue primarily through e-mail that consisted mainly of discussions about our mutual passion for books and some of his thoughts on my sermons. Although he did not believe in the basic premises of the messages, he did find my perspective on Jesus refreshing and much different from most he remembered hearing.

Six months into our friendship he wrote, "I am perhaps the most recalcitrant kind of sinner: an intellectual. . . . There are aspects of my thinking and background that make a leap of faith problematic for me. You are presenting the most convincing argument that I have heard to date."

About a year into our friendship he sent me a very vulnerable e-mail. He and his family had been out of town visiting relatives. On their trip they attended church with his in-laws. He wrote to me on a Sunday afternoon about how offended he was at the "toxic" nature of the sermon he had heard that morning. The sermon, he believed, contained a lot of finger pointing, name calling, and judging of those outside the church. He was mainly writing me to thank me for the contrast that he sensed between the tone of my preaching and the preaching he had heard that morning. "Sinners are like overweight people," he wrote. "They don't need anybody pointing at them and telling them how fat they are; they already know it. . . . My biggest problem with Christianity is Christians."

Then, in a comment I will always cherish, he wrote, "If Jesus came to save anybody (and I know you believe he did), he came to save the sinners, the lepers, the paralytics, not the rich, the smug, those secure in the stronghold of their unassailable faith. If I come around to accepting any Jesus as savior (and I may), I want to know the Jesus that had compassion for the poor, the disenfranchised, the powerless, those with questionable status or darker skin. If I have listened well to what you are trying to say to the church (and I believe I have), that sounds like the Jesus you are talking about."

Our conversations and e-mail exchanges went on for close to two years when one day, seemingly out of the blue, Ryan showed up in my office and announced, "Scott, I'm 80 percent of the way to becoming a Christian." I was taken aback and immediately asked what his 20 percent of apprehensions were.

"First," he said, "I can't become a Republican." I told him that I was sorry if he got the impression that being a Republican was a requirement for following Jesus and that I knew many faithful Christians who were Republicans, Democrats, Independents, and also non-Americans. He laughed and said, "I knew you would say that. I just wanted to get that out of the way."

He went on to explain his dislike for two doctrines he associated closely with evangelical faith. The first was young earth creationism, and the second was the idea of the rapture and its close link to the return of Christ. He explained that although he taught literature, he was a fan of science and that although he was becoming comfortable believing in a God who is the creator of all things, he was certain the process of creation was more complex and took a longer period of time than what young earth creationists taught. I assured him that the statement of faith about creation for our denomination is simply that God created. How God created was up for debate within the fellowship of believers. Our only required belief is that God is indeed the creator. As a church we only reject theories of creation that exclude God as the creator. So I assured him that although he might meet believers from our church who were indeed young earth creationists (I have a friend who is convinced that the first day of creation is October 23, 4004 BC), he would also meet faithful members of the church who would label themselves as theistic evolutionists.

Likewise, I affirmed his concerns about an eschatology that amounted to not much more than, in Ryan's words, "God sucking all of the believers out of the world in order to blow the place up." Here, too, I told him, our church has a very simple statement of faith. We believe that Jesus will return and fully establish his kingdom, but how that happens and when that will take place is debated within the family of faith. Although there are many premillennialist Christians in the denomination, I let him know that many of our members—including many of the church's founders—are postmillennialists (a view much closer to Ryan's own ideas about Christ's return).

After assuring him that his 20 percent was not a deal breaker, I asked him to describe the 80 percent he had come to believe. Ryan proceeded to give me a beautiful description of his newfound faith in a God who created all things and loved Ryan enough to forgive his many sins, who sent his Son not only as a demonstration of his love but as the revelation of the kingdom of God in the world, and who through the power of his presence (his Spirit) now wanted to work on transforming Ryan into a reflection of the nature and character of Jesus.

Ryan's articulate and beautiful description of faith caused me to tear up. He asked me why I was crying. I responded, "Ryan, I hate to break this to you, but you may already be a Christian. In fact, you may be one of the better Christians at this church."

He smirked and replied, "You know, Scott. I have thought the same thing for some time now." We laughed. And then we prayed together.

Ryan was baptized as a brother in Jesus Christ last Easter. Although the conversation above took place right before the church's baptism time at Christmas, Ryan chose to wait until Easter Sunday to be baptized. He explained his reasoning to me this way, "I'm going to wait until Easter to be baptized because when my friends, family, and colleagues find out that an atheist like me is going to get baptized, it needs to be a production, and only Easter Sunday is worthy of this kind of transformation." I was recently at Ryan's home for dinner, and on the mantle is a framed picture of his baptism with his certificate of baptism (also framed) next to it. I jokingly called it his "shrine to the unthinkable."

What follows is an interview between Ryan and me about his days before faith. Although Ryan's parents brought him to church as a child, he spent most of his teenage through adult years fluctuating between agnosticism and atheism. I asked him to answer the questions with his old life in mind. Typical of Ryan, before the interview he did some reading. To fairly represent the viewpoint of the atheist he read two or three of the books that are part of what has been described as the "new atheism." In particular, Ryan read through Christopher Hitchens's book *God Is Not*

Great: How Religion Poisons Everything[1] and *The End of Faith: Religion, Terror, and the Future of Reason* by Sam Harris.[2]

After reading these books, Ryan believed that the authors represented well his own beliefs before coming to Christ. Ryan found that much like his own assessment of Christianity, the books were not indictments of the tenets of faith as much as they were judgments of the misuse of religion by the established church. In Ryan's words, "Hitchens has the same problem I had. It isn't that he rejects Jesus. Like me, he finds Jesus quite intriguing. He hates Christians and in particular the religious establishment that operate as guardians and bullies in the culture."

Ryan continues to struggle with many aspects of faith. Although he has committed himself to Jesus as a disciple, many questions still plague him. But he often says to me, "Faith that wrestles daily with a multitude of doubts is much greater than what gets called faith but is in actuality ignorance parading as certainty."

Questions About Worldview

SCOTT: Describe to me the worldview of the agnostic or the atheist.

RYAN: Personally, I generally believe that humankind desires to do good, although some people choose to do great evil. People tend to be generous and giving when they have plenty of goods, and conservative and stingy during times of scarcity.

It sounds crass to label it simply as a materialistic worldview of supply and demand. But I have sort of a reactionary or impulsive view of human nature. It's easier for people to be nice when they have more stuff than they need.

SCOTT: What do you generally think of as the meaning of life?

RYAN: The purpose of life is to do meaningful, beneficial work with the days given to you. John Locke described it as "enlightened self-interest." When a person contributes to society, that individual usually receives prosperity, security, happiness, and peace in return. And on the flip side, when a person does not contribute [he or she] receives little in return.

When an individual fulfills his or her responsibilities and social roles, the family, community, nation, and world benefit.

SCOTT: Is there anything that you consider unique about humankind in comparison with other species?

RYAN: I have always considered humans unique in that they possess reason. Animals, on the other hand, are governed by instinct and natural law. This is where the issues of nature versus nurture come into play for me. Humans, like animals, are highly influenced by nature, yet humans uniquely can choose (because of a biological complexity that grants to us free will), whereas animals cannot.

Questions About Ethics

SCOTT: What do you believe the good life looks like?

RYAN: The good life looks like taking care of the interests and happiness of oneself, one's family, one's community, perhaps one's nation, but not at the expense of others. I often tell my students that my goal in life is to do more good than harm. A good life is one of civic, moral, and fiscal responsibility.

SCOTT: Do you have a code of ethics that you live by?

RYAN: I believe that people should live a life of honesty, trust, love, caring, fidelity, loyalty, and truth. I do think there is something about human beings that finds goodness and happiness in fidelity to family and to one's neighbors. In short, I think the Golden Rule is a good code of ethics.

SCOTT: Where do these ethical principles come from?

RYAN: Certainly they are principles that are taught (at least in part). Parents, teachers, politicians, society, [and so on], should pass down these civic values from generation to generation. This will sound strange coming from an agnostic/atheist, but I think even the church performs a helpful service here. Many agnostics/atheists believe that if there is a value to religion, it is as a social construct that transfers principles and core beliefs of a culture to the succeeding generations.

But even though I think of the systems that pass on these values as social constructs, I believe they are constructs that are passing on values that are at least partially inherent or part of the nature of people.

SCOTT: So you like the moral values of the church?

RYAN: I didn't say that. What I said was that the church does its most important work when it is helping to reaffirm the general values that society affirms are latent within each person. When the church is damaging society is when it is imposing specific, and often trivial, moral precepts upon people and a culture that may or may not share its cultural convictions and social location.

SCOTT: What drew you to literature?

RYAN: Even though I do not believe that there is a God who has given to the world some purpose or meaning, I do still wrestle with existential questions of meaning and purpose for life. I think I have been drawn to literature because I see great authors trying to imaginatively wrestle with the questions of meaning.

SCOTT: But that meaning is ultimately arbitrary?

RYAN: At some level yes. Nietzsche is right that at times we need to fight against systems that try to will their power in society. But I guess part of me believes that there is an inherent meaning to life and that we need authors, philosophers, and artists constantly dialoguing about what that meaning is and helping people to embrace it.

Questions About Christianity

SCOTT: What is your view of Christians?

RYAN: Christians are people who believe that their creed is right and all other sets of beliefs are wrong. Christians believe that salvation—or heaven—can only be obtained by accepting Christ as a personal Savior.

Christian religion is often used as a bludgeon against "sinners" and/or nonbelievers. The whole perspective of Christians divides "us" against "them." Exclusivity, judgment, self-righteousness, and a general lack of compassion are the hallmarks of mainstream evangelical Christianity.

Most of my friends whom I would also consider to be atheists/agnostics feel that most Christians reek of hypocrisy and arrogance. They do not generally consider Christians fun people to be around. They see Christians primarily as hypocritical, perhaps even unfairly so.

SCOTT: But what do you think about Jesus?

RYAN: I believe that Jesus was an exemplary man and teacher. He was probably also a great prophet, and by that I mean he was a great social theorist in his day, but he is one of many great leaders in world history.

Unfortunately, I do not see Christians concerned with following his example and teachings. I see them . . . concerned with maintaining their social constructions and religious institutions rather than really paying attention to Jesus.

SCOTT: What's your perspective on the Bible?

RYAN: The Bible is an interesting collection of ancient literature, much of which, like all great literature, is trying to make some meaning out of life. In my view, it is important to consider the ancient culture the Bible emerged from before applying isolated verses wholesale to modern conduct. Not only can Scripture be skewed and lack context, but such practices can also be reductionistic and even dangerous. Most people have the skills to make the Bible say just about whatever they want it to say.

The discussion of the Bible as literature could be a point of unification, but because it is usually proof-texted, and thus able to be used for a personal agenda, it is usually more of a club for pounding against another's view than a potential tool for uniting.

SCOTT: What in particular bothers you about the Christian faith?

RYAN: I can't stand Christians' sense of unassailable certainty.

For example, I went to a funeral a couple of days ago for a friend and local businessman. He had a massive heart attack and was dead before he hit the floor. He was only fifty-five years old, which is only five years older than I am. Unexpected deaths always make me ponder my own mortality.

It was a large service with four hundred or so people in attendance. The pastor gave the kind of eulogy that the audience expected. "Even though he was rarely in church," proclaimed the pastor, "So-and-so was baptized here, married here, and so he is with God now."

A Christian leader from my town was sitting in front of me. I greeted him after the service, and we exchanged pleasantries.

Then he said, very matter-of-factly, "Well, he is with God now." Maybe it was the delivery, but the comment bothered me greatly.

It typified much of what I think about Christianity. It is an answer that is too pat and too ritualistic. Both the memorial service and comment left me questioning.

There are many things on my list of things that drive me crazy about Christians, but I think this is the highest complaint on my list: absolute certainty. Too many Christians speak as if they have a lock on heaven and on universal truth. They think that only Christians who believe in their particular way and express their beliefs in a certain way are the ones who will get their "ticket punched."

My question is: How do these Christians know? Have they died and come back? I find the whole thing too smug and too exclusionary. It is as though Christians enjoy defining the boundaries between "us and them."

I realize that it is very hard for most people to live with ambiguity. But in the case of something so unknown—like the afterlife—it seems that some level of ambiguity is unavoidable. How can any of us know for certain what happens after our physical death? It strikes me as a bit arrogant to assume that if there is a God . . . you have the ability to discern what God's perfect judgments are.

I refuse to live my life based on the promise of heaven after death. My goal is to live the best life I can even though I recognize that I am deeply flawed. If there is a heaven and I somehow am good enough to get in, then so be it. If not, well, it was never my call anyway. God gets to do what God gets to do. I'm fine with the ambiguity. I just wish that more Christians would focus on trying to make this world a better place rather than investing so much time and energy thinking about the next one.

seven Listening to Muslims
s Fletcher L. Tink

The Muslim religion (also known as Islam) is, next to Christianity (2.1 billion adherents; 33 percent of the world population), the religion with the most followers in the world, with some 1.5 billion people (or 23 percent of the world population) claiming its faith, according to researcher David Barrett.[1] Also, aside from Christianity, it is the religion most dispersed throughout the world, with over fifty nations in the Middle East, northern Africa, and Asia recording majority Muslim populations. Yet there are many different forms of the faith, primarily Sunni (90 percent of all Muslims) and Shiite, representing different histories, selective influences, and varied cultural settings. Moreover, according to the Carnegie Endowment for International Peace in 2007, it is growing at the rate of 1.84 percent a year compared to Christianity at 1.32 percent, due in large part to the increased size of Muslim families, though the raw numerical growth is roughly the same.[2]

Because of immigration to the West, proselytizing in prisons, the heightened sensitivities to the Muslim presence since 9/11, and the business enterprises of Black Muslims in their communities, Islam is a religion that must command our interest and dialogue.

The core beliefs are universal among Muslims, centered around the five pillars or duties of Islam: the shahadah, that is, the "submission" by the declaration that there is only one God (Allah) and that his prophet is Muhammad; the salah, the required rituals of prayer five times daily; the zakah, or the giving of alms; the sawm, the fast required during the twenty-eight days of Ramadan; and the hajj, the pilgrimage, at least once in a lifetime, to the holy city of Mecca. The use of the Arabic language in prayers and rituals provides universal access that unites otherwise different cultures. The pillars, themselves, make practice for many believers much more accessible than the theological underpinnings contained in the Qur'an. Yet beyond these practices and core beliefs, there are a great many flavors to the religion. In much the same way that no one Christian represents all Christians, no single Muslim can speak for all Muslims. And even within the Muslim faith a variety of feelings and opinions exist about "fringe" and "fundamentalist" Muslims who seem to capture many of the headlines in the West.

For this reason, I was privileged to engage three different Muslims for my interview. I met Dr. Daud and Talat Ashai on a plane ride. They and their two children impressed me with their thoughtfulness and family discipline. Recognizing that they were not American born, I inquired and learned that they were a husband and wife from Pakistan who had immigrated to the United States some twenty years earlier to study. Currently, Dr. Ashai practices medicine, serving as the head of emergency services at a major Fort Worth hospital. Thus he is not a professional or trained Muslim religious authority but like many Muslims has been deeply influenced by his family and national culture. His wife, Talat, also volunteered to respond to the questions posed, giving a unique woman's perspective to the discussion.

Abijah Zabihullah is a Muslim imam, or holy man, given the responsibility of teaching fellow Muslims. An imam is an Islamic leader within a local mosque, leading prayers and teaching. Unlike Christian professionals, there is no formal seminary or denominational credentialing for imams. However, a devotee who studies extensively the Qur'an and practices the religion with integrity is acknowledged by a local mosque for his unique spiritual authority.

I had met Abijah in a religious program at Leavenworth Penitentiary where I headed up the Protestant version of discipleship that ran parallel to the Muslim version that Abijah led. I have always found him to be a gracious, thoughtful man. Abijah was born in America in 1968 as Robert Stewart Jr. He grew up as a Christian and attended the Baptist church in the suburbs and the black Pentecostal urban church regularly on Sundays and throughout the week. A graduate of Jackson State University in 1991 with a degree in criminal justice, Abijah became a convert to the Islamic faith. Though he does not have formal religious training, he adheres to the beliefs and practices of the Salaf al-Saaleh (righteous ancestors of the Muslim nation), holding tenets that are adhered to in the kingdom of Saudi Arabia. Though he is African-American, he is not a Black Muslim, a sect disavowed by the traditional Muslim community.

Questions About Belief System and Worldview

FLETCHER: What is the most important thing in your life as a Muslim?

DAUD: To believe in Allah (God), that he has no son and no father and that the prophet Muhammad is the last prophet.

TALAT: My faith.

ABIJAH: The most important thing in my life as a Muslim is knowledge about my Lord and Creator. This knowledge is essential because the purpose of my life is to worship my Creator. "I have not created the jinn* and humankind but to (know and) worship Me (exclusively)" (Qur'an 51:56).[3] And although a Muslim believes that everything has rights (people, property, animals, environment, etc.), a Muslim believes the great right belongs to Allah, [because] everything exists and is sustained by him. The prophet Muhammad once said to one of his companions, "Do you know what Allah's right upon His slaves is?" His companion said, "Allah and His messenger know better." The prophet said, "To worship Him alone and join none in worship with Him." Then the prophet said, "Do you know what their right is upon Him?" The man answered, "Allah and His messenger know better." The prophet said not to punish them if they did so (Sahih Bukari 9:470).[4] So a Muslim should worship precisely the way the prophet Muhammad allowed, without any deviation [from] that, so the how, when, and where should be followed exactly. We learn this information from his companions in the first three generations of the Muslim nation, so this worship encompasses belief in Allah, prayer, fasting, charity, pilgrimage, and supplications.

---

*Evil demons possessing supernatural powers they can bestow on persons who have the ability to summon them

FLETCHER: **What is the purpose of life? Why are we here?**

DAUD: To live in a simple and humble way. To respect elders and help the needy.

TALAT: To do good and to contribute to the world.

ABIJAH: We are here because of God's plan for humankind to ponder, to reflect upon his creations, to improve it, and to make one's contribution to it, and above all to thank him and worship him in every act of living.

FLETCHER: **How do you worship? What does worship mean to you?**

DAUD: We worship by praying. Worship has a broad meaning. Anything good that you do is worship.

TALAT: There are many ways to worship. When we reflect upon God's creations, we worship him. When we feel thankful to him for every blessing and every creation, we worship him. If I do my job honestly and contribute to humanity in some small way, I feel it is my way of worship.

ABIJAH: Worship encompasses belief in Allah, prayer, fasting, charity, pilgrimage, and supplications. Worship means everything, and nothing comes before it whether [that be] relationships, careers, hobbies, and so on. So a Muslim's love for Allah is the greatest love. A Muslim believes in Allah the way [Allah] describes himself by his glorious names and perfect attributes [that] he revealed through his messenger.

FLETCHER: **What do you believe about God, human freedom, the natural world, and human relationships?**

DAUD: There is only one God. Human freedom is extremely important. There is a lot of emphasis on good relationships.

TALAT: I believe that God is One and the Supreme Creator.

An individual human being has been given a free will to make the choices in life. However, every action and every choice has some "consequences" that are beyond one's control. So in a way human freedom has its limitations.

The natural world is indifferent to individual life. On the other hand, I feel that human actions do have an impact on the natural world. Human indifference toward the environment will eventually bear its consequences for humankind and may seriously endanger it.

How people conduct themselves in their relationships is the ultimate test of their values and their worldview. It is in how they deal with each other that we see the best of humanity or its worst.

ABIJAH: As far as where Allah is, we believe he is above the seventh heaven over his throne. "Indeed your lord is Allah, Who created the heavens and the earth in Six Days, and then He *istawa* (rose over) the Throne (really in a manner that suits his majesty)" (Qur'an 7:54).[5] To put the throne in perspective, the prophet said that the *kursi*, or footstool that is beneath the throne, extends over the entire universe or cosmos and that this footstool compared to the throne is like a ring thrown out upon an open space in the desert. The prophet said, concerning the size of the angels that guard the throne, that the distance between the earlobe and shoulder would require five hundred years of travel for the human being. Therefore, the Muslim believes that Allah is outside of his creation and that there is nothing physically above him.

With regard to human freedom, we believe that humans as well as jinn have been given the ability of choice to decide if they will submit to their lord and cherisher. As far as the natural world, we believe that every created thing praises and glorifies its sustainer and that there is no option or choice for them. This would also include the angels.

With regard to human relationships, we follow the instruction from the prophet to discharge the appropriate rights of good treatment, fairness, and justice.

FLETCHER: Why do you believe the way you do?

DAUD: From the teaching of the religion.

TALAT: I was raised in a religious family. However, as an adult I went through my own spiritual quest. I questioned and finally formed my own worldview after several years of questioning.

ABIJAH: As Muslims we believe that Allah communicated his will through his messengers and that all of these messengers came with the same message: to worship Allah alone and none else (Qur'an 12:40). This message has never changed from one messenger to the next.

FLETCHER: What happens when you die?

DAUD: You will be judged by your deeds.

TALAT: I believe in life after death.

ABIJAH: Muslims believe that when [someone] dies, angels come and interrogate the person on three matters: (1) Who is your Lord? (2) What is your religion? (3) Who was your prophet? Then the individual is either given comfort or punishment [depending on the] response to these questions. This continues until the day of judgment. The rewards or punishments in the grave are proportionate to the individual's deeds in this life. Going to heaven or hell immediately after death is not a Muslim belief. Those destinations are reserved for the final judgment day.

Questions About Lifestyle

FLETCHER: **How do your beliefs influence your daily life?**

DAUD: Beliefs do influence daily life. They help one to stay away from evil things.

TALAT: In my daily life I try to be always conscious of the presence of God. On the one hand, it prevents me from a lot of evils like lying, cheating, and so on; on the other hand, it encourages me to be always fair, honest, and kind toward others.

ABIJAH: My belief influences every aspect of my daily life. Earlier I mentioned that prayers of protection are a part of worship. The prophet specified certain duties [or prayers] before or after certain actions—upon waking up or going to sleep, before eating and drinking, before intercourse and going to and from the bathroom, upon riding as well as ascending or descending, upon experiencing hardships or hearing thunder, and countless other remembrances. As Muslims, we are encouraged to follow the prophet in these [prayers to remind] us [of our Lord in a unique way at] every moment of consciousness. Through these prayers, one is engaged in direct interaction with forces that could cause one harm. For example, the prophet stated that the jinn's nature is to inhabit filthy areas like bathrooms, so the prophet would pray before going into one by saying, "O Allah, I seek refuge in you from the male and female [devils]."[6] By making these utterances, a person becomes aware of dangers that he cannot see and is therefore able to avoid them, if Allah so wills it. All of the prophet's prayers have some goal and aim that he was seeking to accomplish, because he was given knowledge of the unseen dangers.

FLETCHER: **What does it mean to live a good life?**

DAUD: It means to live a life that is balanced in all aspects.

TALAT: In my opinion a good life is the one that gives a sense of fulfillment, is productive, [and] contributes to humanity in some way.

ABIJAH: The prophet said, "The deeds of any one of you will not save you from the fire." They said, "Not even you, O messenger of Allah?" He responded, "No, not even me unless and until Allah bestows his mercy on me and protects me with his grace. Therefore, do good deeds properly, sincerely, and moderately" (see Sahih Bukari 8:470). In addition, what is good is defined by Allah and communicated through his chosen messengers.

Questions About Ethics

FLETCHER: **How do your beliefs affect your relationships with others?**

DAUD: They don't, really.

TALAT: My beliefs always prompt me to do the right thing.

ABIJAH: Treat all persons with gentleness, fairness, and justice, with an emphasis on justice even if it goes against my own personal interests.

FLETCHER: **What ethical principles do you live by?**

DAUD: Principles such as those based on respect, equality, and fairness.

TALAT: I believe in the principles of truthfulness, honesty, fairness, justice, and kindness.

ABIJAH: I try to worship Allah as though I see him. But since I cannot see him, I know that he sees me. This knowledge is enough to [shy me away] from doing anything that might displease him.

FLETCHER: **What effect do your choices have on your destiny?**

DAUD: A lot.

TALAT: Generally I feel that [humans make choices that] do shape their own destiny and the destiny of their children. At the same time I do often think about the fortune or the misfortune of being born in a certain place or a certain way. But even then we have certain choices available to us that are relative to our situation in life.

ABIJAH: Choices do have an impact but only from the angle of earning pleasure or anger from my Lord. I cannot by myself bring about a good or bad end for myself. It is only through earning my Lord's favor that I can inherit bliss. Of course, I would like to help myself by making good choices. But the end result is with Allah.

FLETCHER: **What principles or rules, if any, do you think are basic to living?**

DAUD: To me, religious principles are basic to living.

TALAT: Truthfulness, honesty, fairness, justice, and kindness.

ABIJAH: The prophet said, "Love for your brother what you would love for yourself."[7]

FLETCHER: **How do you decide what is right or wrong in any situation?**

DAUD: Using common sense.

TALAT: I follow my gut feeling about it. I also try to look into my personal worldview and my religious view.

ABIJAH: Here, we refer back to the Qur'an and the speech and actions of the prophet that can be authenticated. Therefore, knowledge of religion is the most beneficial knowledge.

FLETCHER: **Where do you draw the line when making choices involving others?**

DAUD: I don't draw any lines.

TALAT: It is a highly relative question. Generally I would try to think what is best for them if they are incapable of making their own choices. If they are capable of making their own choices, I can only make suggestions and then back off.

ABIJAH: Because of the ability of choice, man receives what he deserves. If he is obedient, he receives abundant blessings and security. But if he is disobedient, he earns evil and misery through his own hands.

FLETCHER: **Why do bad things happen to good people?**

DAUD: It happens. Sometimes it happens more to good people. One belief that we use to comfort ourselves is that God sometimes tests his favorite people more.

TALAT: As a Muslim I have learned that the two most important attributes in life are thankfulness and patience—thankfulness to God even in the worst situations and patience in the times of trials. I feel good people are often tested in their [lives] for these two attributes. It is not hard to bear bad things if one has a strong faith in God and in the life after death.

ABIJAH: Pain and suffering [are] intended to lead a person to humility and repentance by which he can redeem himself and rectify his situation. This "bump in the road" is a mercy from his Lord. For if one [were] only rewarded for doing evil, one would never change from that course. When one would finally meet his Lord, Allah would have to punish him because of [Allah's] perfect character of justice. But if one would find that the road of evil leads to misery, one would be more apt to change for his own salvation as well as for others.

FLETCHER: **What do you think about the idea of checks and balances in the universe? A final judgment or karma?**
DAUD: I think very strongly about it.
TALAT: I do believe that there will be a final judgment based on fairness and justice.
ABIJAH: As for a final judgment day, this is one of the six pillars that constitute Islamic faith.* The others include belief in Allah, his angels, his divine revelations, his messengers, and his divine decree. According to the prophet, on judgment day, the people will be raised up naked, barefooted, and uncircumcised. The sun will be brought close to the earth, causing severe thirst. And the people will look to earlier prophets for intercession. The scales will be brought forth so that the deeds of humankind can be weighed and a bridge will be laid over the hellfire in which all believers must cross. This bridge, as thin as a hair or razor, has sharp hooks that snatch up sinful people.

Questions about Christianity

FLETCHER: **What do you think Christians believe?**
DAUD: They believe in Jesus and God.
TALAT: Generally I think Christianity believes in the concept of the original sin, the Trinity, and the Savior. Apart from that, I believe that Christianity and Islam both have a lot of common teachings.

---

*These six pillars of faith are distinct from the five pillars of practice mentioned earlier.

ABIJAH: I understand that because of Adam's breach of his covenant, all his offspring fell out of union with their Creator. To reharmonize this union, the Creator sent his Son to die for this transgression, and only a perfect sacrifice could accomplish this. To have faith in this message is tantamount to achieving success in the next life.

FLETCHER: **What experiences have you had with Christians?**

DAUD: Good experiences.

TALAT: I have had mostly good experiences with Christians. They are very helpful, generally good people.

ABIJAH: I've had both pleasant and unpleasant experiences. I believe this holds true for all people, regardless of their religion.

FLETCHER: **How does Christianity compare with what you believe?**

DAUD: They are both very similar.

TALAT: The story of Islam also begins with the story of Adam and Eve as in Christianity. However, I believe that they were forgiven for their sin. We are here on this earth by divine design. Each individual is born innocent. In our adult life the choices we make determine what kind of life we will have in this world and in the hereafter. I believe that God sent his messengers from time to time for human guidance. I do not believe in the divinity of Jesus (peace be upon him), but I believe in his virgin birth and in his prophethood, as in the prophethood of others before him and the prophethood of Muhammad (peace be upon him) after him.

ABIJAH: The comparisons between Christianity and Islam are too numerous to elaborate. But for the most part the sharia

(Islamic law) and Christian legal systems are very close in comparison. Economic principles on usury (the charging of interest), as was practiced by early Christians, is the same as Islamic social codes in dealing with others on the basis of kindness, fairness, and justice.

FLETCHER: **What do you think about Christianity?**

DAUD: I think very highly about Christianity. I have to believe in Christianity to be a Muslim.

TALAT: It is a great religion. As a Muslim we have to believe in the three divine religions (as we call them): Judaism, Christianity, and Islam.

FLETCHER: **What do you think about Christians?**

DAUD: I believe them to be good people.

TALAT: We call them the People of the Book, as are Jews and Muslims. We also call [these religions] the Abrahamic religions, as they all start from him. Muslims are supposed to pray five times a day. In every prayer we send blessings to all the children of Abraham.

ABIJAH: I view them in the same way as I view all human beings, with dignity and respect. I believe they have the right to believe in the Creator in any manner that suits them and that my dealings with them should be upright and noble.

FLETCHER: **What do you think about Jesus and his teachings?**

DAUD: I believe them to be good.

TALAT: Jesus is one of the great prophets of God. The Qur'an has a whole chapter titled "Surah Maryam [Mary]," which tells us about the miracle birth of Jesus. It tells about his childhood and how he spoke from his cradle in defense of his virgin mother. The Qur'an tells us about his miracles when he grew up and started to spread the Word of God. Like all prophets, he teaches about God and godliness.

ABIJAH: I have nothing but love for him and his mother and the utmost respect for his teachings. However, I do not believe he is God or even the Son of God or part of a Trinity with God, for a Muslim should not believe that God eats or drinks, [since this] causes one to eliminate waste [and] no impurity can be attributed to Allah. [Nor can it be said] that he sleeps or takes rest, for no deficiency can be attributed to Allah. If one sleeps, then one cannot be all aware and cognizant. All these qualities are unique to the creation and its creatures but not for its Creator, who is above such things.

Author's Response

I was delighted with the willingness of my friends, two new ones and one, Abijah, whom I have known over five years, to respond so kindly and enthusiastically to my questions. I found their answers to be consistent with my impressions and knowledge of them.

Each is soft-spoken, thoughtful, and gracious, quite different from the caricatures that the media might impose on us. The Ashais, like many immigrants, are delighted and thankful for the opportunities that this country affords and are living successfully and contributing much to the overall culture. Their religious perspectives are deeply embedded and are part of the legacy of their own history. To deny their "Muslim-ness" would be to deny a part of their own history.

^{ight} Listening to Buddhists
^e Kim Lundell

Buddhism is an Asian religion. It not only was conceived in Asia but also developed historically and spread geographically in almost every nation of Asia. It is a system offering an explanation of the ideal universal human life. It endeavors to explain this life, the next life, and the cause-and-effect principle affecting this life. Richard A. Gard, a Buddhist writer, observes in the introduction to his book *Buddhism*, "[Buddhism] offers any individual or society a voluntary way of thought and conduct, based upon an analysis of conditional existence, dependent upon supreme human effort, and directed toward the realization of freedom in perfect existence."[1]

Buddhism is a way of life in most Asian nations, where it is characterized by ethnic diversity and possesses great socioeconomic influence.

Buddhism can be roughly divided into two schools. First, Mahayana, the "greater vehicle," has by far the largest number of adherents. Its features include the participation of common people, idol worship, chanting, and an emphasis on compassion. Pure Land, Nichiren, and Tibetan are well-known expressions of the more religious form of this school of Buddhism. Within Mahayana is Hinayana, the "lesser vehicle," which is by contrast austere, demanding greater effort and emphasizing meditation. It tends to be more intellectual, of which Zen Buddhism is a well-known expression. Mahayana is practiced primarily in China, Japan, Korea, Tibet, and Vietnam.

The second group or school, actually the older, more original, is Theravada, "the teaching of the elders." Theravada emphasizes the continuous analysis of life rather than the following of ethics, faith, or rituals. Theravada is practiced primarily in Sri Lanka, Thailand, Burma, Cambodia, and Laos. Despite the differences with those practicing Mahayana, Theravada adherents also hold to the Four Noble Truths (see interview below) and are very similar in their basic philosophies and daily practices.

Most Buddhist laypeople are unable to distinguish the differences between the two schools or articulate what the exact beliefs are. For the sake of clarity in this discussion, I will follow the categories of Mahayana.

I live in a Chinese community where I have made several Chinese friends. Almost all of them say they are Buddhists. But when I questioned them about Buddhism, none of them could pinpoint what they believe; they only gave me vague answers. For example, when I asked, "What is the most important thing in your life as a Buddhist?" One answered, "Being a nice person and almsgiving to help the Buddhist temple and poor people to invoke the blessing for the sake of me and my family members." They were not sure about Buddhist doctrine or theology. They said, "Buddhism is not a religion, but it's a philosophy." Gard says:

Most Westerners or non-Buddhists tend to view and define Buddhism as a philosophy, noting its humanistic concern with right action being based upon right knowledge, or as a religion, perceiving the frequent incorporation of folk religious beliefs and practices in its institutional development. But "philosophy" and "religion" are primarily Western concepts which have had various meanings in the course of Western thought. . . . Buddhism may be described as a philosophic interpretation and religious expression of a way of life, Asian in origin but intended to be universally human in outlook.[2]

And my Chinese friend Evan Chu said Buddhism is not a religion but a philosophy and traditional Chinese way of life, which means she does not separate religion and philosophy.

Along with my Chinese friends, I asked several Koreans about their Buddhist faith. Three are brand-new Christians, with each representing a different age or occupation. Young Ae Ahn is a seventy-two-year-old grandmother whose granddaughter is a committed Christian; she has lived as a Buddhist most of her life. Young Won is a twenty-nine-year-old Korean man FOB (fresh off the boat) who attends a language school to prepare for American college life. Min Sun is a twenty-seven-year-old mother who has been a Christian for two weeks. I myself was born and raised in a Korean Buddhist home for over thirty years, so I knew what they were talking about.

(Note to the reader: The following interview includes a combination of composite and individual responses. Individuals are

identified when their specific answers are given. Otherwise the answers recounted are the composite responses of several interviewees or comments by the author.)

Questions About Belief System and Worldview

QUESTION: **What is the most important thing in your life as a Buddhist?**

ANSWER: To obtain dharma. *Dharma* is the Sanskrit word that means "hold." It is the teaching of the Buddha. And the Buddha state is the state of enlightenment. Dharma is the package of Buddha's teaching and refers to any practice through which a life has its continuum held back from a specific fright or suffering. This holding back or protection can be from sufferings, which are effects, or from the causes of those sufferings, the afflictive emotions. We are seeking to control the mind, and those practices through which the mind is controlled are dharma.

Dharma leads to the great Enlightenment of self-realization through the thirty-seven teachings of Enlightenment, grouped as follows: the Four Foundations of Mindfulness, the Four Exertions, the Four Bases of Psychic Power, the Five Faculties, the Five Spiritual Powers, the Seven Factors of Enlightenment, and the Noble Eightfold Path.

From a very wide point of view, the word *dharma* is like a vast jeweled net where every jewel is set perfectly and contains and reflects the image of every other jewel. The Four Noble Truths and the Noble Eightfold Path are the first ever teachings of Buddha on dharma.[3] The Four Noble Truths identify the problems.

The First Noble Truth is dissatisfaction—that humans are never satisfied.

The Second Noble Truth is the cause—craving. We are never satisfied, and we want more due to our craving. The Third Noble Truth is cessation of the cravings—which also brings cessation of dissatisfaction. This is what Buddha saw on the night of Enlightenment: that the endless cycle of birth and death is driven by insatiable cravings, which constantly entice. He could never live with satisfaction. When all the bonds of craving dropped away, he was free with no more constrictions or limits.

The Fourth Noble Truth asserts that there is a path that leads us to the cessation of cravings: the Eightfold Path. The Eightfold Path is Perfect Vision, Perfect Emotion, Perfect Speech, Perfect Action, Perfect Livelihood, Perfect Effort, Perfect Awareness, and Perfect Samadhi [see glossary].[4]

QUESTION: **What is the purpose of life? Why are you here?**

ANSWER: Evan Chu responded: "I think why I am here is the result of cause and effect, which is reincarnation of my former life. I must have done good to be reborn as a human being, not as an insect or animal."

When asked about the vision and purpose of her life as a Buddhist, Evan Chu said she had none. "I just want to make it in society and have a successful career and life." Buddhism is a prevalent phenomenon in belief and practice, yet it does not provide theological or concrete answers to grassroots questions about evil or salvation.

Buddhists are on a journey that takes them through the cycle of birth and death. A person is not here by accident; he or she is here due to the causes and actions of his or her former life. A life is nothing but a series of becoming through cause and effect. That is a person's karma. Karma is the cosmic power of cause and effect; it is an idea that understands present conditions to be the result of past causes. Naturally, life consists of streams of becoming. It's cyclical, like a spinning wheel; once it begins, it continues to turn.

QUESTION: **How do you worship? What does worship mean to you?**

ANSWER: Young Ae Ahn said, "I worship Buddhist sutra [teaching from ancient texts], reading and hearing Buddha's teaching from the priest and reciting the simple incantations. Also I bow down before Buddha's statue a thousand times in his temple and offer alms to support the Buddhist temple. Reading Buddha's teaching (dharma) calms my heart when I am troubled or worried. And by bowing to Buddha and keeping the amulets and talisman I believe I will receive financial prosperity and protection from evil, disaster, and danger. Listening to Buddhist monks' teaching, I change the attitudes of my life. I also chant the name Namu Amitabha, and I also bow to the Bodhisattva spirit [see glossary for both terms]."

Buddhists all over the world recite and contemplate in their daily exercises the nine sublime virtues and rituals contained in Pali formulas. They prostrate themselves before the statues of Buddha a thousand times to worship him and meditate, recite the sutras and mantras, express gratitude, and act on Buddha's teaching of compassion.

Another devotional practice is self-transcendence. Buddhist meditations, called *samatha*, are performed to control the mind. All worship is related to a person's dharma and karma. Worship means one must reach what a Mahayana Buddhist calls the *anatta* non-ego state of Buddha nature. It is the state of non-self in which egocentricity, not human personality, is denied. The denied self is the true self, and God is within your real self. A person acquires this state through meditation.

QUESTION: **How often do you go to the Buddhist temple?**

ANSWER: Young Ae Ahn and Min Sun said April eighth (Buddha's birthday), July seventh (alignment of stars), August fifteenth (harvest), New Years Day (for blessings on the new year), and the middle of each month for the devout. They offer incense, offerings, and bows.

QUESTION: **What do you believe about God, human freedom, the natural world, and human relationships?**

ANSWER NO. 1: Evan Chu answered, "We believe in only one supreme God. For the Westerner he is Jesus, and for the Oriental he is Buddha. We think he is the same god. We are free when we empty ourselves from internal greed and evil desire. We should be considerate toward other people and be kind to them in order to go to paradise and for rebirth as human beings in a good family afterlife."

ANSWER NO. 2: Since we are to control this world and ourselves, there is no creator or supreme being. We are the creators of ourselves, that is, the enlightened selves. We are to know that we live by delusions, because life is a process of becoming. It is not God's creation but our creation within ourselves through the process of becoming. Human freedom comes from attaining the state of Buddha, which is the embodiment of the great virtues; it is the enlightenment of realizing our true self, free from all delusions and cycles of birth and death. The process is as follows: Because of ignorance, volitional activities arise; because of consciousness, mind and matter arise; because of mind and matter, six senses arise; because of six senses, cravings arise; because of cravings, attachment arises; because of attachment, karma condition arises; because of karma, birth arises; because of birth, old age and death arise. Naturally if the cause ceases, the effect will also cease. If ignorance can be completely eradicated, that will lead in stages to the cessation of birth and death.

Buddhism was introduced to Korea in 57 BC, primarily through two Buddhist sects: Hinayana, which developed Son (Zen) Buddhism, and Mahayana, called *Chongtojong* (Pure Land). The Son sect emphasizes meditation (the very word *Son* means "meditation"). Pure Land Buddhism teaches that one can obtain salvation (Pure Land) by reciting or praying to the Bodhisattva spirit. Pure Land Buddhism does not give comfort in this world but instead preaches rebirth into the paradise of the next world. This sect appealed to the grassroots population and became the largest sect in the Silla Dynasty. Pure Land appealed to the masses, because it did not require knowledge of sutras but offered the simple method of chanting the name of the Bodhisattva spirit and provided hope to those who were burdened and suffering. It was enough to profess one's faith in Amitabha Buddha by citing Namu Amitabha Buddha.[5]

To achieve the Great Enlightenment and ascetic self-discipline, many people renounced secular life. Thus arose Sangha, communities of monks and monasticism. One can discover one's true self in Sangha by practicing fasting, praying, meditation, vegetarianism, chanting mantras, and celibacy.[6]

QUESTION: Why do you believe the way you do?

Answer No. 1: Sook Kim, a Korean, answered, "I practice what I have received from my parents and ancestors. Buddhism was the beliefs of our ancestors for over three thousand years. Since it is the traditional religion of my ancestors, I follow their footsteps."

Answer No. 2: K. Sri Dhammananda wrote, "In [Buddha] was the embodiment of highest morality (*Sila*), deepest concentration (*Samadhi*) and penetrative wisdom (*Panna*)—qualities unsurpassed and unparalleled in human history."[7] According to Malalasekera, "Buddhism puts salvation or [nirvana] completely within the reach of man. It does not, however, come to him as a gift from outside himself; it has to be won."[8] In Buddhism there is no Savior who takes upon himself the sins of others and from whom one receives redemption. One has to win the true wisdom and truth of self and life by meditation.

Question: **Can you say something about meditation and the mantra sound?**

Answer: With regard to mantras that one can observe in meditation, there are external sounds of repetition and internal sounds of mental repetition. There are also natural self-arisen sounds, such as the inhalation of breath. In Pure Land Buddhism the word *Bodhi* means "enlightened." There are three stages of Enlightenment: enlightenment of hearers, enlightenment of the self-awakened, and enlightenment of Buddhas.

Question: **Do you believe in an afterlife?**

Answer: "Reincarnation," Evan Chu answered without hesitation. When asked if she really believed that she could be born as an insect or animal, she said, "Yes."

QUESTION: **What do you believe about the afterlife?**

ANSWER: Buddhism explains life as being the continuum of rebirth. The afterlife is continuing the effect of this life. This life causes the afterlife, and the afterlife revolves back into this life, as effected according to the cosmic law of karma, as Gautama Siddhartha (the Buddha) discovered.

QUESTION: **What happens when you die?**

ANSWER NO. 1: Mi Young Park, who is Korean, responded, "I will have an afterlife according to the cycle of birth and death of life. All the natural world around me is in my control. Since through karma, a being is reborn in the course of transmigration (samsara), the being continues in a series of births and rebirths here or elsewhere. According to my own deeds (karma) I will have rebirth."

ANSWER NO. 2: Evan Chu said, "If I am good, I will go to paradise and I will be reborn as a human being in a good family situation. But I am not sure whether I would be good enough."

Questions About Lifestyle

QUESTION: **How do your beliefs influence your daily life?**

ANSWER: Evan Chu said, "I try to be kind and good to other people in order to enter into paradise and for reincarnation as a human being not an animal. I try to practice self-denial and make an effort to give to the poor. Occasionally I go to a temple to a hear monk's teaching and offer incense."

Buddhists discipline themselves to develop a proper Bodhi mind by eliminating the false self and delusions and by meditating on Buddha's teaching of the Four Noble Truths and the Eightfold Path, which leads them into self-realization and enlightenment. Self-realization comes as the result of emptying the self, reaching the cessation of carnal desires, and attaining the enlightened state (Bodhi mind)—and thus attain karmic perfection and freedom from the continuation of cause and effect in this life and the life to come. It leads Buddhists to awaken and develop the Bodhi mind. A Bodhisattva makes four vows:

1. Sentient beings are numberless; I vow to save them.
2. Afflictions are inexhaustible; I vow to end them all.
3. Dharma doors are boundless; I vow to master them all.
4. Buddhahood is unsurpassable; I vow to attain it.

Therefore, Buddhists need to recite the above verses.

QUESTION: What does it mean to live a good life?

ANSWER NO. 1: A good life is to awaken Bodhi mind. The word *Bodhi* means "enlightened" and comes from the same root as *Buddha* and *Bodhisattva*—an enlightened sentient being. The Bodhi mind is the root, and the life is the fruit. In order to attain Bodhi mind, we should meditate and contemplate six critical points:

1. Enlightened mind
2. Mind of compassion
3. Equanimity and respect
4. Mind of joy
5. Mind of repentance and vows
6. The mind of no retreat

To live a good life is to live in the realm of Buddha nature, to die as a small being moment after moment. When we lose balance, we die, but at the same time we develop ourselves and we grow to control ourselves. Shunryu Suzuki observes, "To give your sheep or cow a large, spacious meadow is the way to control him."[9] Suzuki goes on to say, "Because we enjoy all aspects of life as an unfolding of big mind, we do not care for any excessive joy. So we have imperturbable composure."[10]

ANSWER NO. 2: Evan Chu answered, "Living a good life means to have prosperity, success, wealth, health, and longevity."

Questions About Ethics

QUESTION: **What is karma?**

ANSWER: Kulananda writes that "the fundamental Buddhistic teaching is the doctrine of conditionality. Everything arises in dependence of conditions, nothing has a fixed and final essence—and this includes ourselves."[11] This means the result of our former life becomes our present life. As we do, we become. Our behavior is the pattern of rebirth again and again. The wheel of life is turning around and around from the karmic level to the dharmic level.

Our behavior conditions our being and is the essence of Buddhist ethics, an ethics of intention. Buddhism does not think in terms of right or wrong. "Buddhism distinguishes between 'natural morality' and 'conventional morality.'"[12] Conventional morality is a group's rules and customs. Natural morality is "based on the facts of human psychology and the operation of the Law of Karma" and concerns spiritually beneficial outcomes.[13]

QUESTION: **What rules, if any, do you think are basic to living?**

ANSWER: Buddhist teaching is not specific or concrete for every situation. But it is said we should not have a greedy heart. We should realize the truth, which is emptiness of this world. It's because this world is a shadow, a vanity and not a true reality. Our true lives are the realization of ourselves to be in the state of Buddha by meditating and looking within ourselves to find true self. We don't have any special rules, but we try not to kill other animals, and when we prepare to go to the Buddhist temple, we stay away from meat of any kind.

QUESTION: **What ethical principles do you live by?**

ANSWER: The renowned Tibetan Dalai Lama lectured on Buddhist ethics to his Zen society in New York as follows:

To be good followers of Buddha we must mainly practice compassion and honesty. Showing kindness to others, we can learn to be less selfish; sharing the sufferings of others, we will develop more concern for the welfare of beings. This is the basic teaching. . . .

Buddha always emphasized a balance of wisdom and compassion; a good brain and a good heart should work together. Placing importance just on the intellect and ignoring the heart can create more problems and more suffering in the world. On the other hand, if we emphasize only the heart and ignore the brain, then there is not much difference between humans and animals. These two must be developed in balance, and when they are, the result is material progress accompanied by good spiritual development. Heart and mind working in harmony will yield a truly peaceful and friendly human family.[14]

When the Dalai Lama also gave a special lecture at Brown University, he said, "Pleasure and pain come from your own former actions (*karma*). Thus, it is easy to explain karma in one short sentence: If you act well, things will be good, and if you act badly, things will be bad."[15]

This means humans are the masters of their own thinking and actions. In other words, you and I are the kings or masters in control of our own lives. When we control our minds well, we will do good, which will positively affect the next life.

Buddhists are not concerned with rules or commandments, and nobody demands or watches over us to make sure we keep the precepts. One has to adopt them entirely by one's own volition. Different Buddhists adopt different sets of precepts. But the Five Precepts, translated from Pali, are the most commonly used:

I undertake the training principle to abstain from killing. Buddhists take killing as a separation from living. Therefore if we kill, we deprive others. Buddhists not only refrain from murder but also from violence.

I undertake the training principle to not take what has not been given. We not only should not take another's property but also we should not take their time or energy. We only take what is freely offered. By cultivating generosity, we undo our egocentricity.

I undertake the training principle to abstain from sexual misconduct. With stillness, simplicity and contentment, I purify my body.

I undertake the training principle to refrain from falsehood. With truthful communication, I purify my speech.

I undertake the training principle to abstain from intoxicants. With mindfulness, clear and radiant, I purify my mind. Mental clarity and calmness are the central qualities most highly prized.[16]

At the ethical level, these precepts are simply a group or society's rules of conduct. At the practical level, one is committed to living by the precepts, and although still caught up in samsara and still subject to acts of unskillfulness, one makes consistent efforts to live.

QUESTION: **What effect do your choices have on your destiny?**

ANSWER: Choices of behavior and the cosmic law of cause and effect become most significant. For the choices we make, the karmic cause is generated and the result is inevitable. Our destiny is the consequence of our choices. We are the creators of our own paths according the law of cause and effect. Good, helpful intentions produce good results, while bad (harmful) intentions produce bad results.

QUESTION: **Where do you draw the line when making choices involving others?**

ANSWER: Yoon Hi, who is Korean, said, "My drawing line is almsgiving if I can help them. I can show them Buddha's mercy and kindness."

Only a small percentage of Buddhists participate in any kind of temple activities beyond Buddha's birthday, New Year's, harvest rites, or funeral ceremonies. Thus in practice most Buddhists concentrate on the welfare of their families, their businesses, and themselves.

QUESTION: **Why do bad things happen to good people?**

ANSWER NO. 1: Korean friend Soon Ja Chang said, "It's because of their karma [fate]. According to Buddhist teaching, everything in this world is connected to a person's former life. If a person did not do good things in his [or her] former life, the consequence of the former life is that he [or she] will have bad karma and accidents."

Because of their belief in reincarnation, people will typically ask, "What sin did I do in my former life to deserve this problem?"

ANSWER NO. 2: Our lives are a series of cause and effect. Our action of love produces love, and our hatred reproduces the effect of hatred—as when we throw a stone on a pond and it ripples out. Carefulness and calmness bring the same effect. The cosmic law of karma explains that bad things happen as an effect of former actions. The wheel of life is turning. Even when bad things happen to good people, their situation will not stay bad but will teach them to tolerate and master suffering by way of dharma Enlightenment.

In exchange for the belief in self and consequent suffering, Buddha offered peace, joy, and, as soon as one was able to follow the Eightfold Path, extinguishing of the self and absorption into nirvana. *Nirvana* means "blowing out," "extinguishing," and the state of being free from passions (particularly cravings and anger) and consequent suffering.

Buddha taught that individuals could gain enlightenment through the process of self-realization. Anyone can become Buddha, one who is equal in nature to a god. Buddhism considers supernatural powers intrinsic to human nature. Through systematic methods of self-realization, supernatural potential is cultivated and utilized. These methods include celibacy, fasting, meditation, praying, and chanting.

QUESTION: What do you think of the idea of checks and balances in the universe?

ANSWER: Mi Ja Joo, who is Korean, answered, "There is no final judgment. Life is an endless cycle of turning wheels, and karma is all connected through millions of years of reincarnation."

Questions About Christianity

QUESTION: What do you think Christians believe?

ANSWER: Korean friend Seon Hi Choi responded, "You believe God through Jesus; we believe God through Buddha."

QUESTION: How does Christianity compare with what you believe?

ANSWER: Seon Hi also said, "I am not sure, but I don't think we have to go to temple every Sunday."

QUESTION: What do think about Christianity?

ANSWER: Young Ae Ahn said, "I thought that Christianity was a Western religion, that the Supreme God was one, and that Christianity and Buddhism were ways to God. I thought Christians were generally kind and nice people. They looked happy and loving. Therefore, I had a good impression when my Christian granddaughter began to attend a church. Christianity is good."

QUESTION: What do you think about Christians?

ANSWER: In Ja Kim, who is Korean, said, "I think Christians are different from people in the world. The Christians I know are very kind, honest, peaceful, and joyful. They are always loving and caring people and ready to extend their hands to assist others."

QUESTION: What experiences have you had with Christians?

ANSWER NO. 1: Gina Choi, who is Chinese, observed, "I have very positive experiences from my daughter and granddaughter who are totally changed after they became Christian and joined a church. Their lives have been totally transformed."

ANSWER NO. 2: Evan Chu said, "I have several Christian acquaintances through my business. They are all kind and caring people. I believe we serve the same God through different ways."

Glossary

Amitabha—The most commonly used name for the Buddha of Infinite Light and Infinite Life. This is a transhistorical Buddha venerated by all Mahayana schools. Amitabha Buddha at the highest level represents the true mind, the self-nature, common to the Buddhas and sentient beings—all encompassing.

Attachment—In the Four Noble Truths, Buddha Gautama taught that attachment to self is the root cause of suffering.

Awakening vs. Enlightenment—The distinction between awakening to the Way of Enlightenment versus actually attaining Enlightenment.

Bodhi—The Sanskrit word for "enlightenment."

Bodhi mind or Bodhi spirit—The spirit of Enlightenment.

Bodhisattva—One who aspires to supreme Enlightenment and Buddhahood for himself or herself and all beings.

Buddha nature—Means and includes dharma body, true mind, true self, emptiness, nirvana.

Delusion—Ignorance, the belief in something that contradicts true reality or lacks awareness of true nature.

Dharma—Sanskrit for "hold." The whole package of teachings of the Buddhas.

Dharma nature—The intrinsic nature of Enlightenment, emptiness, reality.

Diamond sutra—A sutra that cuts unnecessary concepts and brings one to the shore of Enlightenment.

Eight Sufferings—Birth, old age, disease, death, separation from loved ones, meeting with the uncongenial, unfulfilled wishes, suffering associated with the five raging skhanda.

Five Skhanda—"Components" or "aggregates." The Five Skhanda represent body and mind. The Five Skhanda are form (physical body), feeling, conception, impulse, and consciousness.

Karma—Universal law of cause and effect in all creation that occurs when action leads to future retribution or reward in an endless cycle of rebirth.

Namu Amitabha—See Amitabha.

Pure Land—Generic term for the realm of a Buddha.

Pure Land School—When Mahayana spread Buddhism to China, Buddhism flourished and formed the Lotus Society and branched out into other sects as well. It was well developed as Jodo Shinshu in Japan and as Chongtojong in Korea.

Samadhi—Tranquillity and contemplation.

Samsara—The cycle of rebirth.

Tathagata—Translated "thus come one," the path leading to Supreme Enlightenment, to Buddhahood.

Zen—A major school of Mahayana Buddhism with several branches. One of the most popular techniques is meditation.

Conclusion

So after "listening in" on the different conversations, what are you thinking? Did the exchange between Darrel and Scott in the first chapter leave you pondering how your own faith walk compares with Scott's perception of Christianity? Have you been reflecting on the several concepts of mortality and life after death that surfaced in the discussions? What did you think about Scott Daniel's conversation with Ryan, or Jim Wick's incredibly cerebral but personal interaction with his friend Jim?

As I said in the introduction, we live in a world that is often at an impasse when it comes to communication. Many times this is because we do not really listen to each other when we talk. We filter what we hear through our own biases and screen out much of what a person is saying. Sometimes we even shut our ears while we devise responses we feel sure will persuade others to our way of thinking.

Learning to listen well is a matter of courtesy, but it is also something else. It is a way to align ourselves more closely with the example of Christ. When we allow the Holy Spirit to free us of our preconceptions so we can truly hear the hearts of other people, we will open the door to many possibilities. Friendship, understanding, and encouragement are just some of the possible results of authentic listening.

Listening to others does not mean giving up our value system or compromising our commitment to Christ. But it does mean giving up our desire to dominate our interactions with others.

Listening is Christlike humility in action; it is an attempt to truly understand another person and discern what God is doing in his or her life. Though Christ came to declare in words and actions that he was the Messiah who came to save us from our sins, he also modeled what it means to listen. From his conversation with Nicodemus to his discerning words of grace with the woman at the well (see John 3—4), Christ genuinely heard the hearts of people. With the Holy Spirit's help, that is what we must endeavor to do as well.

So let's begin a ministry of listening. Let's listen at the coffee shop, in the church lobbies, underneath car hoods, and over bowls of spaghetti so that we can get to know our neighbor better, model Christ's humility, and allow the Holy Spirit to give us sensitive ears and kind hearts. Maybe we will even find an opening to ask, "What do you think about Jesus?" But if we don't, we must still display Jesus' love in all our encounters, especially when we listen to those who struggle with life's meaning or who tread religious paths in directions far different from our own.

Notes

Chapter 1
1. Ralph Waldo Emerson, *Essays, Lectures, and Orations* (London: William S. Orr and Co., 1848), 107.

2. "Humanism and Its Aspirations: Humanist Manifesto III, a Successor to the Humanist Manifesto of 1933," American Humanist Association, http://www.americanhumanist.org/Who_We_Are/About_Humanism/Humanist_Manifesto_III (accessed June 8, 2010).

3. Richard Dawkins, *The God Delusion* (New York: Houghton Mifflin Co, 2006), 51.

Chapter 3
1. *The Purpose of Life* (Salt Lake City: Church of Jesus Christ of Latter-Day Saints, 1991), 9.

2. Bruce R. McConkie, *Mormon Doctrine* (Salt Lake City: Publishers Press, 1986), 43-44.

3. Joseph Smith, "Articles of Faith," Church of Jesus Christ of Latter-day Saints, art. 2, http://www.mormon.org/mormonorg/eng/basic-beliefs/membership-in-christ-s-church/articles-of-faith (accessed April 27, 2010).

4. Joseph Smith, *Book of Mormon* (Salt Lake City: Church of Jesus Christ of Latter-day Saints, 1986), Moroni 10:4.

5. Gordon B. Hinckley, *What of the Mormons?* (Salt Lake City: Church of Jesus Christ of Latter-Day Saints, 1982), 6.

6. McConkie, *Mormon Doctrine*, 589. *Man: His Origin and Destiny* is a book by Joseph Fielding Smith (Salt Lake City: Deseret Book Co., 1954).

7. Ibid., 116-17. "D. & C." refers to the LDS book *Doctrine and Covenants*, which is one of several publications that form the Mormon collection of authoritative writings.

8. Smith, *Book of Mormon*, 2 Nephi 25:23.

9. McConkie, *Mormon Doctrine*, 684.

10. Philippians 4:8, according to the wording found in Smith, "Articles of Faith," art. 13.

11. Ibid., arts. 1-13.

12. Smith, *Book of Mormon*, Moroni 7:16.

13. Ibid., Alma 34:32.

14. *Doctrine and Covenants*, Church of Jesus Christ of Latter-day Saints, 88:41, http://scriptures.lds.org/en/dc/88 (accessed April 27, 2010).

15. McConkie, *Mormon Doctrine*, 751. "Teachings" refers to the book *Teachings of the Prophet Joseph* by Joseph Fielding Smith, church historian and tenth president of the LDS Church (Salt Lake City: Deseret Book Co., 1938); "Abra." refers to the book of Abraham from the *Pearl of Great Price*, which is included among the Mormon authoritative writings.

Chapter 4

1. In an embryo, a neural-tube is a hollow structure from which the brain and spinal cord form. A defect in the neural-tube can lead to congenital abnormalities such as spina bifida.

Spina bifida is a defect of the spine consisting of a gap in the backbone exposing the spinal cord and its protective membranes. This defect can cause paralysis and sometimes mental disability.

Chapter 5

1. Robert W. Welkos and Joel Sappell, "Defectors Recount Lives of Hard Work, Punishment," *Los Angeles Times*, June 26, 2009, http://www.latimes.com/news/local/la-scientology062690,0,6177596.story (accessed June 7, 2010).

2. Richard Behar, "The Thriving Cult of Greed and Power," *Time*, May 6, 1991, http://www.cs.cmu.edu/~dst/Fishman/time-behar.html (accessed April 28, 2010).

3. Ibid.
4. Ibid.
5. Ibid.
6. Ibid.
7. Ibid.

Chapter 6

1. Christopher Hitchens, *God Is Not Great: How Religion Poisons Everything* (New York: Twelve, 2007).

2. Sam Harris, *The End of Faith: Religion, Terror, and the Future of Reason* (New York: W. W. Norton and Co., 2004).

Chapter 7

1. David B. Barrett, Todd M. Johnson, and Peter F. Crossing, "Christian World Communions: Five Overviews of Global Christianity, AD 1800–2025," *International Bulletin of Missionary Research*, January 2009, 25-32.

2. "The List: The World's Fastest-Growing Religions," *Foreign Policy*, May 14, 2007, http://www.foreignpolicy.com/articles/2007/05/13/the_list_the_worlds_fastest_growing_religions (accessed June 8, 2010).

3. *The Holy Quran*, trans. Ali Ünal, http://www.mquran.org/content/category/2/51/4/50/50/ (accessed June 8, 2010).

4. *Summarized Sahih Al-Bukhari*, trans. Muhammad Muhsin Khan (Riyadh: Darussalam Publishing).

5. Quoted from the *Quran* in "Allah's Rose Above the Throne," Harari Darul Arqam, http://hararidarularqum.ethionetlink.com/?option=com_content&view=article&id=67:allahs-rose-above-the-throne&catid=31:general&Itemid=68&fontstyle=f-larger (accessed June 8, 2010).

6. My First Steps in Islam, "Various Supplications, Words of Remembrance, and Islamic Etiquettes," http://1ststepsinislam.com/en/supplications-islamic-etiquettes.aspx (accessed June 22, 2010).

7. Paraphrased from Khaled Abou El Fadl, *The Search for Beauty in Islam: A Conference of the Books* (Lanham, MD: Rowman and Littlefield Publishers, 2006), 77.

Chapter 8

1. Richard A. Gard, *Buddhism* (New York: George Braziller, 1962), 13.
2. Ibid., 14.
3. Kulananda, *Principles of Buddhism* (London: Thorsons, 1996), 18-19.
4. Ibid., 21.
5. In-Gyeong Kim Lundell, *Bridging the Gaps: Contextualization Among Korean Nazarene Churches in America* (New York: Peter Lang, 1995), 53.
6. Ibid., 54.
7. K. Sri Dhammananda, "Great Virtues of the Buddha" in *Gems of Buddhist Wisdom* (Kuala Lumpur, Malaysia: Buddhist Missionary Society, 1996), 119.
8. G. P. Malalasekera, "Buddhism and Problems of the Modern Age" in *Gems of Buddhist Wisdom* (Kuala Lumpur, Malaysia: Buddhist Missionary Society, 2002), 69.
9. Shunryu Suzuki, *Zen Mind, Beginner's Mind*, ed. Trudy Dixon (New York: Weatherhill, 1983), 31.
10. Ibid., 34.
11. Kunlanada, *Principles of Buddhism*, 60.
12. Ibid., 62.
13. Ibid., 62-63.
14. Tenzin Gyatso, the fourteenth Dalai Lama, *Kindness, Clarity, and Insight*, trans. and ed. Jeffrey Hopkins (Ithaca, NY: Snow Lion Publications, 1984), 30-31.
15. Ibid., 26.
16. Kulananda, *Principles of Buddhism*, 65-71.

The community-minded church . . .

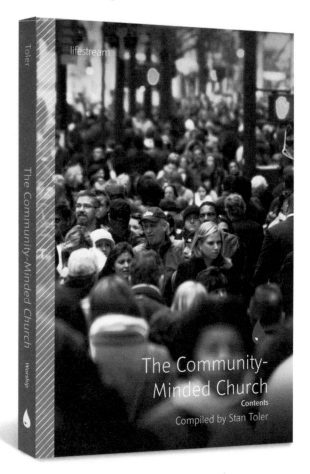

. . . building a community for your community.

Find the right place to spend
meaningful moments practicing
justice and compassion.

Mercy Rising
ISBN 978-0-8341-2497-4